2009

Commandments
of Compassion

A CHURCH BOOK

The **CHURCH** book series from Sheed & Ward focuses on developing discipleship and leadership, fostering faith formation and moral decision making, and enhancing the Church's worship and social ministry. Titles in the series address clergy, laity, and religious on topics and issues that concern the whole people of God.

Series Editor: Karen Sue Smith

Commandments of Compassion

James F. Keenan, S.J.

SHEED & WARD
Franklin, Wisconsin

1999

Sheed & Ward
7373 South Lovers Lane Road
Franklin, Wisconsin 53132
1-800-266-5564

Printed in the United States of America

Cover and interior design: GrafixStudio, Inc.

Permissions:
"On Giving Moral Advice," reprinted from *America*, March 2, 1996, with permission of America Press Inc., 106 West 56th Street, New York, NY 10019. Ph: 212-581-4640.
© 1999. All Rights Reserved. www.americapress.org.
"Moral Theology Today," reprinted from *Priests and People*, October, 1994, with permission.

Library of Congress Cataloging-in-Publication Data

Keenan, James F.
        Commandments of compassion / by James F. Keenan
            p.   cm.
        ISBN 1-58051-060-4 (pbk.)
        1. Ten commandments—Criticism, interpretation, etc. 2. Christian ethics—Catholic authors. I. Title
    BV4655.K44 1999
    241.5'2—dc21
                                                                                    99-34143
                                                                                    CIP

1 2 3 4 5 / 02 01 00 99

CONTENTS

To Jeannine

ACKNOWLEDGMENTS

After I finished writing *Virtues for Ordinary Christians,* my previous book in this CHURCH book series with Sheed & Ward, I wanted to explore a theology that could embody a Christian morality while promoting a Christian spirituality. In my search I returned to the Ten Commandments and began writing about them in my CHURCH magazine column. In the introduction of this book, I explain how it is that our spirituality is developed and advanced in the Ten Commandments—the decalogue—and then present the commandments as well as some other essays that I hope you find helpful and enjoyable.

In putting this collection together, I have edited each previously published essay to eliminate redundancy and to give the collection greater integration. I hope you find it adequate. I have added two previously unpublished essays and am grateful to CHURCH, *Priests and People,* and *America* for letting me revisit my earlier essays.

I want to thank Jeremy Langford, the editor-in-chief of Sheed & Ward, for taking me on board with this collection. I am especially grateful to my friend and editor at CHURCH, Karen Sue Smith, who improved each of my essays with her keen comments. Similarly my community, colleagues, and students at Weston Jesuit School of Theology provided me with such wonderful support and insight that I am sure, without them, I could never have done these essays. Likewise, I was able to edit this book and write a few remaining essays thanks to the generosity of Cleveland's John Carroll University, which provided me the Walter and Mary Tuohy Chair of Interreligious Studies for the spring semester, 1999. Finally, I am indebted to the readers of my column in CHURCH who encourage me greatly.

In these essays I try to bring the insights of fundamental moral theology from their more technical, academic context into ordinary Church life. To achieve this goal I weave narratives from contemporary literature and film as well as from the lives of the saints into my writings. I also talk about myself, my own life of friends and family. Among them is my sister Jeannine who as my youngest sibling brings a lot of love and thoughtfulness into my life. With her husband, Rob, they have also brought into the world their two wonderful daughters, Paige and Jenna. In loving gratitude, I dedicate this collection to Jeannine and her family.

The Ten Commandments as a Gift from God

I teach a course at Weston Jesuit School of Theology called "Introduction to Fundamental Moral Theology." Every year new students tell me that they were originally opposed to taking the course because they thought of moral theology as simply a number of significant actions that the Church finds morally offensive. At the end of the course, the students tell me that they are grateful to have learned that the Catholic moral tradition is richer, more humane, and more intellectually rigorous than they originally thought. Along the way, they are surprised at what they learn.

One of the first eye-opening essays that the students encounter is on the notion of sin in the Bible by scripture scholar Bruce Vawter, called "Missing the Mark." Among his many insights, Vawter demonstrates that the Jewish people never really thought of punishment for their sins as coming from a punishing God. Rather, they saw anything that happened to them after they sinned as an extension or an after-effect of their sin. If they found themselves rejected from the community, for example, for having borne false witness, they believed that the rejection was not a punishment from God, but rather the simple effect of their having borne false witness.

In a manner of speaking, just as the Jews did not believe in punishment as something assigned from God, they also did not believe in reward as something assigned from God. If they prospered it was a natural effect of their right conduct.

This Old Testament way of looking at morality and the world is rather natural and helpful. It makes clear that the moral code for the Jewish people was something naturally helpful to them. The code was not some standard that God set so that God could see who was good or bad in God's eyes. For the Jews God was never like some dog trainer who kept raising the bar and giving a biscuit to each dog that jumped high enough. Rather the law that God gave was a law not primarily for God's benefit and delight, but for humanity's. By the law, we became freer and happier.

In the Christian tradition many theologians have made similar arguments. Thomas Aquinas, for instance, held that nothing bothered God about human conduct except when human beings brought harm on themselves. This was an important insight. What offended God was not really disobedience to the law; God was not like some temperamental lawgiver who became insulted whenever God's wishes and commands were not heeded. Rather, what offended God, Thomas said, was when humanity hurt itself. He believed that our well-being has always been the aim of God's love and wisdom.

For some reason we have lost this crucial insight. We have thought of the law as something "imposed" by God for God's own preferences. Some of us have thought of God's law as an extension of the ego of the law maker who likes to know that God is in command. But God's law is not for God's entertainment; rather, God's law is for our benefit.

THE TEN COMMANDMENTS AS "THE ROCK OF CHRISTIAN ETHICS"

In the history of Christianity, however, the insight that the aim of God's love and wisdom is expressed in law has not been completely lost. For instance, on the eve of and during the Reformation, the Ten Commandments became once again the most important instrument of Christian moral instruction. As they became popular they eventually replaced the seven deadly sins, which for nearly eight centuries dominated the horizon of moral instruction.

As anyone familiar with moral theology knows, the most fundamental moral law has always been to do good and avoid evil. But for a variety of historical reasons that are too complicated to develop here, the Church began from the fifth century to stress the avoidance of sin as the basic moral task and, in the event of failure, confession of one's sins. With the avoidance of wrongdoing as the fundamental moral requirement, the moral task to do the good became merely an elective one.

In order to hear confessions, from the fifth to the sixteenth century priests were helped by certain moral textbooks that assigned the appropriate penance for each sin. These textbooks were called "the penitential manuals" from the fifth to the thirteenth century and after that they were called "the confessional manuals." These texts were organized according to the seven deadly sins—pride, envy, anger, sloth, avarice, gluttony, lust.

In the writings of some fifteenth-century theologians, notably Jean Gerson, an attempt was made to provide a more positive, Scripture-based formation to Christians and to overcome the minimalist claims of simply avoiding sin. Gerson turned to the Ten Commandments, which he called "the rock of Christian Ethics." His main context for the instruction on the Ten Commandments was a "catechism," and he and others began putting together these accessible and somewhat comprehensive books of Christian instruction.

A century later, during the Reformation, Martin Luther and John Calvin and then the Council of Trent (1545–1563) itself also sought out the Ten Commandments as the main basis of moral instruction in the context of catechetical instruction. Their appeal to the decalogue became a strong repudiation of the primacy accorded to the seven deadly sins. First, because the decalogue was in the Scriptures, it, and not the deadly sins, enjoyed the biblical claim of expressing God's will. Second, unlike the seven deadly sins, it offered not only negative prohibitions, but on occasion, positive prescriptions. Finally, with the possible exception of pride, the deadly sins were primarily offensive to human life alone; the commandments specified prescriptions and prohibitions that began with our relationship with God and moved from there to our relationships with one another.

It is helpful to see an example of how the decalogue was used since it appeared in several important sixteenth-century texts. Martin Luther's *Large Catechism* (1529) dedicated nearly half of its one hundred twenty pages to the decalogue. Generally speaking in terms of prohibitions or prescriptions, Luther began his instruction of each commandment by following the specific form of the commandment, but then turned to its corollary. The commandment on killing began, for instance, with an explanation of the prohibition and eventually considered the failure to do good to one's neighbor: "God rightly calls all persons murderers who do not offer counsel and aid to men in need and in peril of body and life." These explanations focused not on particular external actions that were in themselves right or wrong, but rather on interior dispositions and particular relationships. The eighth commandment, for instance, requires "that everyone should help his neighbor maintain his rights." Above all, the heart dominated Luther's interpretation of the decalogue. He concludes the first commandment: "where the heart is right with God and this commandment is kept, fulfillment of all the others will follow of its own accord."

In that same year Luther published the *Small Catechism*—a shorter version than its predecessor—so that the head of the household could instruct the Christian family. The three features seen above—matching prohibition and prescription; emphasizing habitual, relational conduct; and acting always from a charitable heart—were found in each of the Ten Commandments in the smaller version as well. For instance, the eighth commandment is simply: "We should fear and love God so that we do not deceitfully belie, betray, backbite, or slander our neighbor, but apologize for him, speak well of him, and put the most charitable construction on all that he does."

Restoring primacy to the Ten Commandments happened then in every one of the three main denominational movements of the sixteenth century. Roman Catholics and the followers of Martin Luther and John Calvin recognized in the decalogue a moral foundation that was biblically based, had both prescriptions and prohibitions, asserted the priority of the interior disposition over the exterior action, and began with our relationship with God and moved to our relationship with one another. Indeed, the Ten Commandments were recognized again as "the rock of Christian Ethics."

A GIFT FROM GOD

The Ten Commandments are a rock because they express the providential sovereignty of God. When we read the account in Exodus of Moses' reception of the Ten Commandments, we see how clearly the question of God's sovereignty and God's providence are one. Only by recognizing the powerful care of God can the Israelites dedicate themselves trustfully to God's own guidance. And, so God establishes God's own sovereignty in their midst precisely for their benefit.

Obeying and heeding the Ten Commandments is then a way of entering into the presence of our caring and giving God. Like Moses on the mountain, we get a glimpse of our providential God through the Commandments themselves. But that glimpse is only possible for a people of faith who recognize the sovereignty of God and of God's name. It is in doing that we see that only through prayer and with abiding devotion can we grasp the rock of Christian Ethics. From that perspective, too, we return to the original moral task to do good and avoid evil.

The Ten Commandments

CHAPTER ONE

The First Commandment

"I am the Lord your God who brought you out of the land of Egypt, out of the house of bondage. You shall have no gods before me. You shall not make for yourself a graven image, or any likeness of anything that is in heaven above or that is in the earth beneath, or that is in the water under the earth; you shall not bow down and serve them" (Ex 20:2–5).

In order to understand the Ten Commandments, it is key to understand the first, which presents God as mercy; it commands us to recognize that God alone is merciful.

What would you say if I asked you, What is mercy? I have gone around asking my community members, What *is* mercy? Panicked, they look at me as if I'm giving them a test. But test aside, what is mercy? I don't think most of us know. Curiously, when we cry out, Lord have mercy! I would say that we have as much a sense of what mercy is as when we cry out, *Kyrie eleison*. In Greek or in English, mercy is something we ask for, but that's about it. Yet what is it we are asking for?

If I asked, What is justice? people would be able to answer, "to give all persons their due." If I asked, What is compassion? they would say, "to feel with others in their suffering." If I asked about fidelity, they could respond, "strengthening the bonds of one's relationships." But if I ask about mercy, people look at me as if to say, "Now that's a hard question."

Some try to describe mercy in terms of justice. Mercy makes justice less harsh, more sympathetic, humane. "Mercy tempers justice," they say with a sigh of relief, thinking that they have the right answer.

Several theologians point out that when we think of Christian justice we have to see it always in terms of mercy. For instance, they contend that many people have an image of God as judge at our Last Judgment that is like a judge in a contemporary courtroom. The contemporary judge always seeks to be impartial in order to measure objectively the evidence for and against the accused. By contrast, these theologians convincingly argue that God is never impartial; God has already taken sides from the beginning and continues trying to save us at every stage of salvation history. Our God's justice is from its beginning merciful.

RESCUE MISSION

Recently I returned to Italy where I had studied for five years. I went with a good friend to an island (Torcello) north of Venice where the twelfth-century cathedral was recently restored. We were looking at an enormous mosaic of the Last Judgment on the cathedral's back wall. It showed people being torn apart and eaten by animals, people drowning or being put to the sword. There was great violence and in the midst of this, Jesus was standing as Lord of the Judgment.

As we were looking on, an American tourist group arrived, and their leader began explaining the mosaic. She said that it was the Last Judgment, an awful and terrifying day and that the priest would preach about it frightening the congregation into realizing what the horrible events were that awaited them for their sins on the Last Day. My friend and I kept looking at the picture and the more we did, the more we saw. The picture was not, as the tour guide claimed, a picture of Jesus casting people into the terrible punishments of hell. In fact, we found hell tucked away in a little corner of the mosaic with just a few tortured souls. Rather, the majority of the picture was the tragedy of life on earth. Jesus was returning to rescue us on the Last Day, from painful death. Jesus was taking us from the sea, the animals, the sword. He was coming as a saving judge. A few were condemned, but most were being rescued and brought back to life.

I think that rescue captures the meaning of mercy. Mercy is an act of rescue. Its being an act is important because our entire tradition always talks about mercy in terms of actions, as either the spiritual or corporal works of mercy. Like clothing the naked or feeding the hungry, mercy entails acts of rescue, whereby one stretches out to those who are struggling to survive. Understanding mercy as rescue helps us to appreciate the powerful utterances of those with illnesses who cried out, "Jesus, Son of David, have mercy on me." They were crying out to Jesus to rescue them from their blindness, from their leprosy, and from their marginalization by the rest of society.

In a similar way, when we cry out in our sinfulness at the beginning of the liturgy, "Lord, have mercy," we are not crying out to Jesus, "Be not severe in your judgment." Rather we are asking Jesus to rescue us. We are not saying, "Don't punish us, even though we are sinners." We are saying, "Save us *because* we are sinners." We cry to Jesus for his mercy; we want to be rescued like those figures in the mosaic from Torcello.

Jon Sobrino, the well-known liberation theologian, also saw mercy as rescue in his important book, *The Principle of Mercy: Taking the Crucified People from the Cross* (Orbis, 1995). Mercy is the act of God saving us and we are called to imitate God in God's own act of rescue. For that's what the works of mercy are, after all: imitating God as God rescues. It is for this reason that Jesus tells us that at the Last Judgment those who have performed the corporal works of mercy will be saved, for by rescuing others we participate in God's life.

Thomas Aquinas taught that mercy was the act of letting God live and act within us. He wrote that charity had only one action, the action of mercy. Charity is the virtue by which we are united with God. By charity God lives in us, and we are like God when we practice acts of mercy. To practice mercy is to allow God to act within us, for God alone is mercy and love.

But while we might be tempted to think of what we should do, so as to be merciful, I think it is more important for us, in understanding the first commandment, to see just how much God is merciful. We should look not at what we should do, but rather at what God does. Can we recognize the ways that God rescues us? Do we bring to the surface the way that God literally enters our lives to save us? Do we see the hand of God in our own lives?

In order to appreciate the significance of why we need to recognize God's mercy, we can think of the famous response to the ten people with leprosy who cried out, "Jesus, Son of David, have mercy on us." When, after being cured, only the Samaritan returns, Jesus is astonished. He is not astonished because the others are not grateful, but because they do not realize that they have just been touched by the hand of God. Only the Samaritan returns, bows his head into the dust of the ground, and kisses the feet of Jesus. Having been rescued, he does not simply thank Jesus, he recognizes Jesus' Lordship, that Jesus is the Son of David.

To realize that one has encountered mercy is to realize that one has encountered God. Do we today recognize mercy in our own lives? Do we recognize that we have been rescued? Do we realize that we have been saved, maybe not in one dramatic moment, but throughout our whole life long? Do we see the times that the hand of God has been with us, saving us at a variety of turns?

In a beautiful movie, *Tender Mercies,* a widow tries raising her eight-year-old son. He weeps for his father who has died in Vietnam. She tries to care for him and to earn enough money to support them from their run-down gas station. Eventually a drifter comes to town and settles in a room at the station. As time goes on, he helps her with some chores, makes the station more attractive and lucrative, and finally falls in love with her. She in turn heals him. He has a wife and daughter who have left him earlier because of his alcoholism, though now, in this new relationship, he finds sobriety. He still longs for some sort of reconciliation, particularly with his daughter, and, in fact, achieves a modest one.

In the meantime the boy and the man bond, and the widow, a deep Christian believer, wants the man with her son to be baptized. After a baptism by submersion, they are riding home and the man turns to the boy and says, "Do you feel any differently?" "No," replies the boy, "do you?" "Me neither," says the man while smiling to the boy and his mother. She responds, "I just thank God for his tender mercies."

Not surprisingly then the first commandment begins with a narrative reminding us that God rescued us from Egypt. God is merciful and God alone delivers us. Like those who were cured of their leprosy, we are called in that commandment to see that we have been touched by the hand of God. Only that hand saves us.

The first commandment calls us to attention: to wake us up to the history of God's intimate saving actions in our own lives. It calls us to see how God has kept us in being, through God's own merciful hand, guiding, directing, healing, and sustaining us at every turn. It commands us then first to consider God's mercy in our own specific, ordinary lives and then to recognize the Lordship of the One whose tender mercies touch us so concretely. For when we know how well we are rescued, we know that we have encountered God.

CHAPTER TWO

The Second Commandment

*"You shall not take the name of the
Lord your God in vain" (Ex 20:7).*

INVOKING ANOTHER'S NAME IN VAIN

When I was in high school on Long Island, I had several terrific teachers, among them two nuns in math and one in religion. In religion it was Sister Jane who got me thinking more than did any other person during my four years there.

As a high school student, I wanted a lot of attention (all high school students do). One day Sister Jane came into our class to substitute for another teacher; I was in a particularly dreadful mood. When I saw her, for some inexplicable reason I sighed disdainfully and audibly, "Sister Jane." The students around me snickered: someone was mocking the teacher who claimed considerable respect from the entire student body.

She was distributing some papers and when she came to my desk, she said simply, "Thank you." There was nothing sarcastic about her phrase, but there was considerable irony. She was letting me know that she was hurt by what I had just done. She was also in her usual brilliant way calling me to account for it.

Three years later I entered the Jesuits. Like all Jesuit noviciates, it was a two-year program. At the age of seventeen, I was quite excited with what I was doing. After being in the novitiate only a month, I learned that one of my five other class-mates was leaving. On my way to get a cup of coffee down in the dining room, I overheard several of the second-year novices talking: "Did you hear that one of the first-year guys is leaving?" "No! Already?" "Yeah." "Who is it?" "Guess." They all shouted out at once, "Keenan." After being told who was actually leaving, they laughingly discussed why they thought I was the one.

I never entered the dining room that day. I couldn't believe that in an entire group everyone thought that I was the least suitable for the Society. And I couldn't believe how easily they could bad-mouth me. I was hurt.

Many of us have walked into situations like these. We know from experience what such talk does. We know that taking some-one's name in vain makes them the object of entertainment. In short, such talk is ridicule. As I learned from Sister Jane and from my Jesuit classmates, ridiculing someone and being ridiculed are terribly isolating actions: they separate the ridiculer from others and marginalize the one ridiculed. Taking a person's name in vain is nothing other than an attempt at discrediting or dismissing another as not worthy of respect.

INVOKING ANOTHER'S NAME RESPECTFULLY

When we see the force of taking someone's name in vain we are better able to understand the personal significance of uttering a per-son's name. Of course, it is not only in vain that we take someone's name. We also invoke someone's name in order to invest an argu-ment with great authority. In teaching, for instance, a student might ask a question and I might respond something like, "You know, the late theologian Karl Rahner made a similar point." If I say some-thing like that to a student, I make her day.

There are times when we utter a person's name that the utterance is vested with such evident respect. When I invoke any of my col-leagues—such as Richard McCormick, Lisa Cahill, or Richard Gula—I invoke their authority. Their respected name carries their authority.

When I was a student at Weston, my professor of moral theology, Sister Mary Emil Penet, would let us know when we were going into especially difficult material. She would begin with, "I had great difficulty in understanding this material, but when I lived in Rome I asked Father Josef Fuchs for his opinion." We spent the entire semester waiting for yet another episode when Sister Mary Emil would invoke the name of Fuchs.

I ended up going to Rome to meet Fuchs. When I met him, I knew why Sister Mary Emil uttered his name the way she did. The first time I met him was for a scheduled meeting on the steps of the Gregorian University in Rome. He said, "Keenan? Fuchs." I remembered how well that name had resonated in my own theological formation and here I was meeting and discussing the possibility of studying with this great ethicist for the next five years.

Watch, for instance, when a young person recognizes the wisdom of an older person. By the tone alone, we know that this young person holds the older person in great esteem. This tone of respect is practiced by persons in all walks of life. It is clearly evident, just as evident as when we take a person's name in vain: respect and disdain are transculturally expressed in tones!

INVOKING ANOTHER'S NAME LOVINGLY

But there are many other ways of uttering another's name. Consider for instance when you enter someone's office. The phone rings. The person answers. In less than ten seconds you can tell whether the person is talking to boss, employee, colleague, friend, family, or client. The person's tone, interest, and use of the caller's name convey both the nature and the quality of the relationship. The way we speak about another lets others know who, in our own estimation, the person is.

As we age, we become more sensitive to these matters. Now in my mid-forties, I notice an enormous difference between today and years ago in the way I mention a good friend's name. Years ago I took friends for granted. I could easily talk about my friends. Now I treasure my good friends, I do not talk idly about them and I take none for granted. When I utter the name of a friend, people know that this is someone mighty important to me. And, if I am with a group of people and suddenly one begins talking of a friend of mine and begins moving that person's name to the area of entertainment, I often remark, "Excuse me, but she's my friend." There is no way that any of us allows a friend's name to go in any direction that even hints of a lack of respect. We frequently protect the names of our friends.

Listen to the way parents talk about their children. Hear how the parents' affection is expressed in the names of their children. Listen to the tenderness. We are capable, by the simple utterance of a person's name, to communicate the love we have for another person.

INVOKING THE NAME OF THE LORD

How is it, then, that we invoke the name of the Lord? When we utter the name of Jesus, do those around us know who Jesus is for us? Do they recognize that for us (and for them) Jesus is our Savior?

Clearly in our culture today many people invoke the name of the Lord frequently and rarely is that invocation anything but self-serving. Our culture bandies the name of the Lord with incredible abandon and, not surprisingly, refers to our age as the post-Christian world. For by taking the name of the Lord in vain, our culture tries to marginalize the Lord.

Given our culture's callous treatment of the name of Jesus, then, we need now—more than ever—to avoid participating in any way in its attempts to isolate the Lord of history from our world. We must be attentive to the way we invoke the Lord's name.

We must also be attentive to another problem. As several recent writers have noted, our culture quietly marginalizes those who take the name of the Lord seriously. Their message is simple: genuine thinkers do not believe. In the face of that silent but audible message, how do we take the name of the Lord? Does the "sophistication" of the world in any way inhibit what we want to convey when we utter the name of Jesus? Are we intellectuals intimidated by our peers' own quiet attempts to ridicule our faith in the name of the Lord? How much do we tangibly feel muted by their estimation?

Do people know, by the way we use the name of the Lord, that Jesus is the one in whom we place our faith? Do they know that we have in him our hope that we shall one day be reunited with those who have gone before us? Do they know that he is our priest, our friend, our companion, our redeemer?

The second commandment wonderfully reminds us that uttering another's name discloses the speaker's estimation of the one named. From the beginning of our journey in faith, God has invited us to be attentive to the way we voice the Lord's name. Today the same commandment urges us in our ordinary human intercourse to get into the habit of expressing the Lord's name with loving reverence, for our benefit and for our culture's.

CHAPTER THREE

The Third Commandment

"Remember the Sabbath day, to keep it holy. Six days you shall labor, and do all your work; but the seventh day is a day sabbath to the Lord your God; in it you shall not do any work" (Ex 20: 8–10).

STAGE THREE

A famous writer on moral development, Lawrence Kohlberg, held that there were six stages of development for moral reasoning. Each of these stages builds on the previous one: we all begin at the first and a few finally arrive at the sixth. While these stages may at first sound technical, they quickly become very easy to recognize.

At the first stage, for instance, children believe that right conduct is whatever Mom or Dad says. They believe this because Mom and Dad "are in charge": whoever is in charge is right. At the second stage children try to determine right conduct on their own. Sometimes called, "let's make a deal," at this stage children go out with some toys and trade them for others. They attempt to learn what's a "right" trade among their playmates, though some learn better than others.

At the third stage children begin to institutionalize their way of making decisions by joining clubs and teams, for example. Here children do not know why rules are in place; rather, they just learn the rules of the club or team and follow and enforce them. Ask them, "But, why do you run around four bases?" and they say, "It's because that's the way we always do things." Ask them, "But why are there only three outs?" and they answer, "It's because that's the way we always do things."

Adults, too, confront this expression. We ask someone for instance, "But why do we need these forms?" We hear, "It's because that's the way we always do things." We know at that point that it is useless to ask anything else. The response tells us that the respondent has not and will not think about any of this. When I hear those words uttered I usually turn around and say, with a slightly obnoxious twinkle in my eye, "stage three."

Stage three keeps us from recognizing that rules have reasons. When we teach children to follow the signs at a crosswalk, it is not because we always have done it that way, nor because we just want children to obey us. It is because in this way drivers and pedestrians can be equally accommodated in their respective movements. Likewise, a rule requiring children to attend school is not in place to satisfy some rule, but to educate them.

Rules have formative purposes; they exist to shape us. But stage three reasoning keeps us from asking or knowing the purpose behind a rule. To all the "why" questions about rules, the answer "It's because that's the way we always do things" eradicates any grounds for understanding and respecting the existing rules and customs.

To the question, but why do we observe the third commandment, we unfortunately hear the answer, "It's because that's the way we always do things." In fact, no other commandment more frequently gets this response to the "why" question. Children, teenagers, and disaffected Catholics want to know why they have to go to Mass on Sunday. Too often, they hear, "It's because that's the way we always do things." The stage three answer does nothing but insist on authority, albeit God's. Worse, it keeps the formative reason for the third commandment hidden.

REST, CELEBRATION, GATHERING

Understanding the purpose of the third commandment is understanding what God wants for us. That is, like all the commandments, the third one exists because God wishes to form us through it. Just as God gave us the fourth commandment so that we would love and respect our elders and the fifth so that we would live peaceably with one another, God gave us the third commandment so that we would "rest," "celebrate," and "gather." For these reasons God commands us to keep the Lord's day holy.

In the Old Testament, the commandment appears primarily to imitate God, who rested on the Sabbath. One of the most productive scholars here at Weston Jesuit, the New Testament theologian Dan Harrington, ascribes to the third commandment by saying that God wanted us to rest. This man, who writes more books than anyone I know and is dedicated to understanding and teaching the Scriptures, does no work on Sunday. He begins keeping the day holy by worshipping God. He celebrates the liturgy on Sunday precisely to acknowledge that he participates in the rest that God enjoys. This reason for the third commandment then is to teach us to recognize our limits and to enjoy them as God-given.

The second reason is celebration. Interestingly, the early Christians did not rest on Sundays. On the contrary, lest they be understood as idle, they worked as everyone else did. But when they gathered to worship they honored the Lord's day by celebrating it. Here we see, too, that the very meaning for Christians celebrating the Lord's day is through the Eucharist, which itself means "thanksgiving." Through the Eucharist, Christians gather to keep holy the Lord's day, by celebrating in our lives the one who redeemed us by his body and blood and who promises to come again. Our celebration is at once an act of memorial and an act of anticipation: we remember what Jesus Christ has accomplished and we express our expectation of what he pledges. Nothing conveys this more than our response to the consecration in the Eucharistic prayer: "Christ has died, Christ is risen, Christ will come again."

A third reason why God commands us to keep the Lord's day is precisely to gather us together in prayer and ritual. This command, like all God's commands, is God's attempt to shape us, not primarily as individuals, but more importantly as a people. We know this because we know that God gave Moses the tablets not to make each Jew good, but to make the Jewish people God's chosen people.

The commandment is then a call to keep holy the Lord's day through celebrating a communal act. Through that liturgy God calls us into community. When we hesitate to attend the Eucharist on a Sunday we may be tempted by wondering, What can I gain today? But that question is not the right one. The question we ought to entertain is, What can we gain today? By worshiping together on Sunday we say a corporate "yes" to God's command to become a people; the liturgy engages us as church unlike any other action.

LIBERATION

There is a fourth reason underlying the third commandment and it is found by understanding the roots of Christian observance of the commandment. In the first centuries, the church Fathers encouraged participation in the Eucharist and the divine office without invoking the third commandment; the commandment and Sunday worship were not originally considered a perfect match. Sabbath observance was a command to imitate God the creator who rested on the Sabbath; Sunday observance was a celebration of the Lord's death, resurrection, and return. The language of obligation seemed more suitable for mandating rest than celebration. To make Eucharist an obligation was itself a problem: Have you ever *made* someone say "thank you"?

While the early church resisted Sabbath observance, the emperor Constantine imposed Sunday observance by calling for a cessation of all forms of work, except for farming. Then, in the sixth century, the Council of Orleans (538) and later Martin of Braga (d. 580) articulated a prohibition against "servile work." This law was an imposition not on the serfs; they wanted to rest, to celebrate, to be called into community. This law was rather an imposition on those who controlled the serfs: they now had to let their serfs rest, celebrate the Lord's day, and be gathered into the community. The move was extraordinary, for the most marginalized were, through it, brought into communion with the Lord and were educated. They could belong to a community in which they previously had not been free enough to participate. The "obligation" then was a liberating one: Sunday observance signified their freedom. Tangibly, Sunday was a foretaste of the promised freedom of the Lord, who has already freed all of us from sin and death.

Later Thomas Aquinas developed this liberating notion by seeing the Eucharist as celebrating our passage from human servitude to divine service. In the freedom that the serfs encountered we saw with them a call to be freed so as to serve.

Centuries later we would forget all this, particularly why "servile work" was originally prohibited. Instead we developed all sorts of arguments for distinguishing servile work from other forms of permitted work. Servile work no longer meant the work of the serf; it simply meant menial work that should not be done.

Of course behind it all lies the call for the church itself to be hospitable. For the third commandment, in summoning us to observe the Lord's day challenges us to participate in the very nature of God as the Creator who rests, as the Redeemer who celebrates, as the Sanctifier who gathers. In that Triune action we are no longer passive recipients of God's grace, but rather active participants in the Lord's nature *keeping* the Lord's day holy. By the third commandment, we are freed, as Thomas Aquinas says, for service. As the church once had the vision to assure the serfs a place in the church, we have no less a charge today to make the church a place where others encounter a welcome and a dignity not found elsewhere. Therein the Lord's day is truly a day of the new creation.

CHAPTER FOUR

The Fourth Commandment

"Honor your father and your mother,
that your days may be long in the land
which the Lord your God gives you"
(Ex 20:12).

HONOR OR OBEY

Ask almost anyone what the fourth commandment means and the response will be, "obey your parents." Peculiar isn't it? The commandment says, "honor your parents," but we translate it as "obey your parents."

We think the fourth commandment calls us to obey because we learned it that way. The first virtue we were taught was the virtue of obedience. It is the virtue that parents, teachers, and baby-sitters dream and hope every child acquires. Obedience makes a child easier to teach and so the lesson of obedience precedes all others.

By the time we get to the lesson of the Ten Commandments, we have already learned the fourth, but we learn it as "obey." I'm not complaining that early in life we learn a corruption of the fourth commandment. That obedience lesson is an important one and because of it we learn many others.

Today, however, because our parents live longer, we should return to the original language of honor. Until recently, we did not think it ordinary for a family to survive three generations. Now we are moving toward the expectation of at least four generations, if not five. Whereas before children did not even meet their grandparents, now they know their great-grandparents. Now sons and daughters know their parents not only for twenty or thirty years, but fifty or sixty years. Whereas before people knew their parents up until the beginning of their own adulthood and were obedient to them, now we know our parents for decades longer and need to honor them. So, sure, the first fifteen years of our lives, we say that the fourth commandment means "obey your parents," since the best way young children can honor parents is by being obedient. But for the remaining forty or fifty years, we as adults need to honor our parents, as God has commanded us.

HONOR, A VERY ADULT VIRTUE

I learned about honor from my dad. I have to preface this by mentioning that my entering the Jesuits was hardly by my parents' suggestion. Neither parent was terribly keen on me (the first born) leaving home at seventeen. But eventually we all got used to it. When I was ordained twelve years later, I worked for two successive summers at Xavier Church in downtown Manhattan. Every Sunday my dad would make an hourlong drive from Long Island to hear me preach. Later, when I taught at Fordham, he journeyed to the University Church whenever I preached, and when I took a parish call on Long Island, he came there, too. He didn't come to give me extra support or to teach me anything. He came to listen to me. I was honored. It was then that I learned to honor someone by listening to them.

I often listened to him, especially his stories. As a New York City cop and later as a state investigator, my dad told uproariously funny stories of his and others' investigations. He loved to tell them. Underlying these was his compassion; he appreciated the complexity of human life, the poignancy of human suffering, and the comedy of human intercourse. When I would venture into New York, he would talk about the people in his precincts: the rabbis and clergy, the rich and privileged, the poor and abandoned. He would talk about prostitutes whom, he often said, had an acute sense of fairness: they knew human misery and the way things should be. He would tell terrible stories about pimps, hypocrites, and foul-mouthed bullies, people he especially disliked. Through each story I heard his love for the irony of New York City and I saw how he loved falling into the rat race of humanity.

My dad and I had a wonderful relationship, but it wasn't until his last years, and in particular the very last year of his life, that I learned to honor him. A year before he died at the age of sixty-two, he had open-heart surgery. It was at that time I considered his mortality. It was frightening. I told my spiritual director who in turn gave me great advice: "talk with your dad, listen to his stories, learn more about him; you don't know how long you have him."

I learned new stories not only about his work, but about him. On occasion I would ask him what his family was like. I knew his mom, but his dad died before I was born. He would tell me stories of his mom's anxieties and the difficulties they caused him and his sister. He would tell me how poor he and my mom were in their early years of marriage and how they looked for a variety of jobs to supplement his income. There was one childhood story in particular that he told that was lovingly simple. He said that his dad could insist on things that didn't make sense. (This was comical for me, for I had learned from my mom and dad how kind, humorous, and thoughtful my grandfather was.) At breakfast, he would cut up grapefruit, not perpendicular to the sections, as most people do, but rather parallel to them. My dad, my aunt and my grandmother would all try to tell my grandfather that he made it harder to get at the fruit. They would try to show him the more customary way, and then the next morning they'd come to breakfast and he would cut the grapefruit the same way as he had, convinced that he was right. He would let his family tell him how wrong he was, then he'd smile, and then just continue doing it his way. There was nothing great about the story, but it was the meaning it had for my dad: it lovingly framed his father.

After my dad died, my mom began telling me her stories. She talks about the way she changed high schools, the jobs she had and the better ones she found, and her ambitions and her desires to move about. She tells me how she loved working at Saint Francis College, how she and my dad met, how they dated, and how he took piano lessons (stunned me). She talks about death: her dad's during her childhood, her son's, and her husband's.

Her stories are filled with details, more than my dad ever provided. They are above all touching, wonderfully ordinary narratives that tell me more about her than any impressions I ever had. These stories have been alive in her memory and now in my own as well.

I now know how little I really knew my folks. I realize now that all the categories that I created to understand my parents are nothing more than the deep and lasting impressions of a child. I thought I knew them; but I only knew them through the filtered experiences of a child's mind. Even in my adult years I kept seeing their actions as extensions of those same old categories that I so astutely placed my parents in. Finally I realized that the only way I could know them was by listening to them, by no longer presuming that I really knew them so well, and by willingly asking them to tell me about themselves.

BEYOND RECONCILIATION

So much of the literature for my generation and those behind me has rightly helped us deal with the issues of disfunction in our family lives, with the narratives of manipulations, and with the (more than?) residual anger that lingers after childhood. This literature calls us to get in touch with our own histories and with the persons who helped shape those histories. We are called to face, acknowledge and claim them, for better or worse, as our own. In a word, we are called to be reconciled to those stories and those persons, our parents.

These last thirty years of a therapeutic modeling guiding us to personal freedom were shaped by narratives that we knew and experienced. We have for these years told the generations ahead of us what we experienced. We have insisted that they listen to us. But by the fourth commandment we are called to move beyond reconciliation and beyond the narratives that we have analyzed, accepted, and shared. We are called to let those before us now speak again, not as parents commanding obedience, but as adults sharing with us their formative years and their experiences that occurred before we were born.

We are called to become familiar with their memories, so as to honor them. We are invited to know them as they knew us: as children, teenagers, young adults. We are summoned to walk with them as they talk and as they move eventually toward a new childhood of their own.

CHAPTER FIVE

The Fifth Commandment

"You shall not kill" (Ex 20:13).

THE FACE OF A BABY

My nephew, Brandon Keenan, was born ten days ago. His birth was the high point of this year simply because I love the birth and sight of babies, especially those in my family. They bring me incredible happiness.

I remember that my first niece, Megan, was baptized on June 1, 1980. It was a wonderful family affair. All of us were together. Though they had moved to New Hampshire, Megan's parents, my sister Deb and her husband Gary, had gotten permission to have Megan baptized in the Church on Long Island where they were married and where all of us were raised. My brother, Bob, a baker, made a wonderful cheesecake to celebrate the baptism. My sister and her family returned to New Hampshire after dinner that evening. Tragically, the very next day, my brother drowned. My sister Deb flew down with little Megan. Our grief was nearly inconsolable, but the few moments of peace and joy were those when we looked on my niece. She was our life, in the midst of our grief.

When my dad died of a sudden heart attack in 1991, we were similarly comforted. My youngest sister, Jeannine, gave birth to Paige just after Dad's death and as we gathered for Thanksgiving dinner, our hearts were broken. Paige could just look at us, however, and bring us great comfort. She was new life in the midst of grief.

Anyone who has suffered similarly knows the consolation that a young child's face brings. It can truly illuminate our hearts when they are saddened, grieving, anxious, or fearful. I remember in the summer of 1982, having just been ordained, I was preparing to leave for doctoral studies in Rome and was suffering from terrible anxiety. I was barely able, some days, to lift my head. The anxiety was burdensome. But whenever I went walking and saw a baby, in the midst of all my fear, I found consolation.

For all Christians the face of a baby is a wonderful expression of life, because in our tradition, we believe that human life is promise: the promise of God as Creator who has made us in the image of God; the promise of God as Redeemer who has put to death death so that we might live; and, the promise of God as Provider who leads us to imitate the Spirit of God who is provident and protects life. For Christians, life is not simply blood, breath, and flesh: it is the promise of God made visible to us from generation to generation.

This is why, I think, even the coldest among us can be affected by the innocence, fragility, and humanity of a baby's smile. That smile touches our own humanity. George Eliot conveyed this in her luminous *Silas Marner*, the story of a baby who crawled into the miser's life and changed his heart. Babies touch us precisely in our deepest humanity: they awaken us to our vulnerability by their own and, when they smile, they put us at ease with our own very fragile human condition. Their faces help us see the extraordinary beauty of the human condition and they communicate that, not through words, but with their simple gestures. The face of babies gives us a glimpse of the delicate mystery of the human.

THE SANCTITY OF LIFE

As Christians we have always started with the gift of life in order to understand the fifth commandment. Wherever we find the Ten Commandments in Christian writings, whether the new Catechism or the Tridentine one, whether Luther's *Large* or *Small Catechism* or

Calvin's *Institutes*, we always see the Christian tradition's respect for life before engaging the specifics of the commandment's prohibition. We only understand the seriousness of the fifth commandment when we appreciate the sacred importance of human life.

In fact, Pope John Paul II has helped us to appreciate more the sacredness of life by elaborating on that teaching. Prior to his papacy, sanctity of life basically considered human life as God's dominion: what belonged to God was not ours to violate. Simply put, life was God's property; we had no options on it. This use of "sanctity" appeared elsewhere. For instance, the sanctity of marriage meant that Christian marriage was God's bond; we had no right to violate the bond that belonged to God. Likewise, we spoke of the sanctity of the temple. In applying "sanctity" to life, then, sanctity was not derived from anything belonging to our nature: like the sanctity of marriage or of the temple, sanctity derived from the Owner. Gerry Coleman, the previous writer of the CHURCH column on moral theology, wrote eight years ago: "What makes killing forbidden is that it usurps a divine prerogative and violates divine rights." Sacredness rested not on anything intrinsic to the bond, the temple, or life, but rather simply in the fact that they were divine possessions. The fifth commandment was, then, about not violating God's property and sovereignty.

Pope John Paul II expanded on this tradition. Early, in *Celebrate Life* (1979), he signaled his interest: "The Church defends the right to life, not only in regard to the majesty of the Creator, who is the first giver of this life, but also in respect of the essential good of the human person." The Pope suggested that God created *within* the human something that made human life sacred. Later in his encyclical *Donum vitae* (1987) he expanded on this:

> Human life is sacred because from its beginning it involves the 'creative action of God' and it remains forever in a special relationship with the Creator, who is its sole end. God alone is Lord of life from its beginning until its end: no one can in

any circumstance, claim for himself the
right directly to destroy an innocent
human being (Intro., 5).

The Pope brings then the question of God's dominion into play
with us as created persons, not properties in relationship with God.
This passage is in fact key for understanding all his later writings on
life: precisely this text introduces the fifth commandment in the
new *Catechism*.

In his extraordinary encyclical, *Evangelium vitae* (1995), the
Pope develops all further insights on the gift of life and there clearly
breathes life into the sanctity of life argument. He writes: "Man's
life comes from God; it is his gift, his image and imprint, a sharing
in his breath of life" (39). Our lives are, then, a reflection of God's.
Later he adds, "Life is indelibly marked by a truth of its own" (48).
The indelible mark is there from the beginning of every human life.
As the Vatican summary of the encyclical notes, "Precious and fragile, full of promises and threatened by suffering and death, man's life
bears within itself that seed of immortal life planted by the Creator
in the human heart." The Pope provides us then with a theology of
human life that invites us to look into the face of a human being
and to see therein the life touched, shaped, and animated by a loving Creator. Rather than telling us simply what we are against
(abortion, euthanasia, physician-assisted suicide, capital punishment), the Pope gives us reasons from faith why we defend life. He
develops from faith what we experience when we see the face of a
child: we know therein that we see the hand of God who has made
the child in God's image to be with us animated by a spirit that
comes from the breath of God.

WHAT ARE WE FOR?

When it comes to ethics we Catholics often describe ourselves
much more by what we are against than what we are for. That's an
unfortunate habit, because most of our tradition is about certain
wonderful beliefs, like the sacredness of life. We understand the

fifth commandment, then, in a very specific way: we are against killing because it extinguishes, before its time, the human breath that expresses a soul animated by God. We oppose death-dealing practices because we are in awe of the giftedness and promise of life and such practices violate and contradict everything we hope for.

We oppose these activities, then, because we first respect life. This order is important, because without a respect for human life, we are prone to violate it. This claim was made in a recent essay in *The New York Times* which explained how police brutality originates often not out of hate, but out of a failure to respect persons. Police officers who respect human beings, including suspects and criminals, do not tend to brutality; rather those who do not respect the dignity of all persons can become brutal. The attitude of respect is key, therefore, for stemming violence.

The world in which we live is violent. If we want to see less violence, we must not simply oppose actions that deal death; we must promote a respect for life through an understanding of life as sacred. We can do it rather creatively, I think, if we simply ask one another why it is that every human being finds harming the life of a child as the most profoundly repugnant action that we can imagine. The answer that we learn from one another is that we each hold a deeply felt belief in the promise of human life found precisely in its beautiful vulnerability. In that vulnerability, we get a glimpse of the love of our living God.

CHAPTER SIX

The Sixth Commandment

"You shall not commit adultery"
(Ex 20:14).

Ask an ordinary Catholic whether the Church has a positive or negative stance on the human body and invariably you will hear, "Negative." "Negative" is a rather surprising response since the Church's tradition has been intractably invested in the human body since the Church was first established.

Consider, for instance, that the central mystery concerning Jesus Christ is the incarnation! What religion boasts that God became incarnate, that God revealed God's self in human flesh?

Consider, likewise, that our central sacramental celebration is the Eucharist, a thanksgiving meal in which we eat (!) the Body of Christ and drink (!) His Blood. We partake in his life through this sacrament which concretely underlines the incarnateness of God. The Eucharist makes such sense to us because the Incarnation does.

Consider, then, that the overriding promise for all Christians is the resurrection of the body. Through that promise we understand that who we are now is who we will be in glory: we will be glorified in our bodies. The scripture scholar Wayne Meeks makes a similar point quoting Saint Paul: "Christ will be magnified *in my body,* either by life or by death" (Phil 1:20).

The resurrection of the body makes sense when we understand that God continues to love us precisely the way God made us: in our bodies. But that resurrection is established by the resurrection of Jesus: made in the image of God we see in the Risen Jesus our beginning and our end. Michelangelo caught this brilliantly when in painting the famous ceiling of the Sistine Chapel, he depicted the newly created Adam with the same face as the Risen Jesus in the adjoining Last Judgment. The Risen Jesus is the one in whose image we are made!

Consider, finally, how natural for us it is to consider the Church as the Body of Christ. Inasmuch as we are in the Church by Jesus Christ's incarnation, passion, death, and resurrection; inasmuch as by eating his body we are made one in Christ; and inasmuch as we share the same promise of participating in his resurrection, then what we are, Church, ought to be identified with the Body of Christ.

Body, then, is central for understanding Christianity. Through the body we understand God, our worship, our destiny, and our communal identity. For this reason we take our bodies seriously.

Catholics take the appreciation of the body even more seriously. Catholicism, in particular, has elected the visceral as a primary mode of expression. Its emphasis on the sacramental accentuates its regard for the physical, in particular, the human body. Its language, art, and culture are, therefore, extraordinarily corporeal. Think for a minute of the Sistine Chapel, a very Catholic place. I first saw it with a colleague who, after commenting on the ceiling and rear wall frescoes by Michelangelo, showed me the side wall panels by Raphael, Pinturicchio, Ghirlandaio, and others who depicted scenes from the lives of either Moses and the old law or Jesus and the new law. As if to reiterate these frescoes's theme, each is entitled with a word derived from the Latin word for law, *lex*. He remarked, "Here, this is where the cardinals sit and elect the Pope. What goes on in their minds when the only word they see is *law* and the empty throne sitting at the base of Michelangelo's Last Judgment."

I saw something else. I imagined the cardinals sitting there with great nude paintings. They elect the Pope surrounded with images of the flesh, some attractive and some not. Sure there's law, but there is also the most concrete expression of humanity, the nude human body.

Consider, also, our concern for relics, where we locate our attachment to another's holiness precisely through their flesh. In her brilliant book, *The Resurrection of the Body,* Caroline Walker Bynum traces how early and pervasive our concern in relics has been. Through them, we feel accompanied by the saints, whose hair, skin, or clothing we can still touch. Through them, we "preserve" the presence of their holiness.

Clearly, then, as Catholics we take the body seriously. We always have. Saint Paul, for instance, held that the body *(soma)* was so constitutive of being human that the only way we could conceive of the human was as bodily. The body was not something the human being *had*; the body was rather the only way we could understand ourselves.

From Paul to contemporary theologians, we repeatedly see an attentiveness to the human body. Thus, Walter Kasper, in his *Jesus the Christ,* provides an important summary for these reflections on the body.

> According to Scripture the body is so vital to humanity, that a being without a body after death is unthinkable (1 Cor 15.35ff; 2 Cor 5.1ff). For the Hebrew the body is not the tomb of the soul as it is for the Greek *(soma-sema)* and certainly not the principle of evil from which humanity's true self has to set itself free, as it was for the Gnostics. The body is God's creation and it always describes the whole of the human and not just a part. . . . The body is the whole human in relationship to God and humanity. It is human's place of meeting with God and humanity. The body is the possibility and the reality of communication.

If the fifth commandment is about life, the sixth is about the body! It is about appreciating the insight that we are our bodies, that we communicate who we are in our bodies and that the possibility of all our relationships is precisely through our bodies.

We know from the Scriptures of the centrality of God's covenantal relationship with us. From the beginning of the Scriptures, the Word of God reveals God's unswerving fidelity toward us. To be faithful through God's covenant is the invitation we receive from God, and when we reject that offering we are described by God as (in the book of Hosea) a harlot. Not surprisingly, if the body is the "possibility and the reality of communication," then it is precisely as embodied that we understand ourselves as faithful or not. In our bodies, we communicate the truth of our relationships.

The sixth commandment then takes our bodies seriously because the whole Judaic Christian tradition takes it seriously. In so doing, it invites us to realize that the most human of our relationships are those by which we communicate in our bodies exclusive fidelity, for it is as embodied precisely that we can communicate ourselves exclusively.

The sixth commandment stands then as a witness to our relationships and in particular to those relationships by which people are bonded to one another by vows. The sacrament of those vows is that the vowed bodies are dedicated to one another: one is vowed to one's spouse in one's body, just as a religious is vowed to her community by her body. We are vowed in our bodies; nothing could be more Christian or sacramental. By our pledges we take one another's bodies seriously.

The sixth commandment stands as a witness to the fact that it is in our bodies that we declare ourselves for one another. In marriage, this is classically expressed in sexual relations. But when we realize that our relationships depend on our bodies, then we realize that the sixth commandment is not only talking about sexual relations, but also about every corporeal expression. A kiss, a touch, an embrace, and a smile communicate the essence of a variety of relationships. The sixth commandment stands then as a reminder that every time we physically extend ourselves to another we nurture the faithful bonds we share with one another.

It also warns us against any inappropriate expressions. Above all, it warns us that violating our vows is not "just a physical thing." Violating them is an act of betrayal. We can not distinguish our vows from our embodied relationships with one another. But those vows are not only violated by inappropriate sexual activity but also through any physical action that contradicts the vow. A slap, a punch, a sneer, or a shove contradicts any vowed relationship we have. Just as these actions are violations, similarly the failure to extend oneself to one's spouse is an abandonment of that relationship. For the Christian one need not simply leave one's dwelling to abandon one's spouse; rather withholding any evidence of affection, tenderness, care or concern is itself an act contradicting the pledge to one another.

In a manner of speaking the sixth commandment is specifically addressed to married people, but it serves also as a paradigm for all other relationships. For just as the relationship between Christ and the People of God serves as a model for married people, so too married people in the humanity of their relationship to one another serve as a model for all relationships. Evidently married life serves as a model for vowed religious in their similar commitment to chastity, which embodies their commitment to co-religious as well as those with whom and for whom they serve. But it also serves as a sign to their children and their children's children that love shows itself in deeds rather than in words, and that loving deeds are always deeply, physically human ones.

CHAPTER SEVEN

The Seventh Commandment

"You shall not steal" (Ex 20:15).

When we look at the Ten Commandments we discover a certain order. The first three place before us the sovereignty of God, the next five call us to respect one another in a variety of ways. Thus, the fourth commandment calls us to respect our elders; the fifth, human life; the sixth, our bodies; the seventh, our property; and, the eighth, our good name. The last two summon us to look at our deepest desires to see whether there we actually respect the family and propertied lives of our neighbors.

The respect called for in the seventh commandment has generated, until recently, more questions and reflection than almost any other commandment. In fact, by listening to children we can learn rather effectively just how complex it is. For instance, it has been said that the first moral utterance out of a child's mouth is: "that's not fair." We can remember any number of situations where we have heard a child make this extraordinary assertion. This remark is extraordinary because it marks a significant step in moral development when children are able to ethically assess a situation and, surprisingly, most children are able to recognize these inequities at an early age.

That said, children are far more capable of recognizing what is unfair than determining what is fair. Most parents know, as a matter of fact, that they have to lead a child to understand that fairness is not as easy an equation as Mary gets two apples and Linda gets two apples. What happens when you have three apples and a pear! Or worse, what happens when Linda has an allergy to apples! Because assessing what is due to whom is such a complex issue, children are always asking questions about fairness.

A friend of mine, for instance, was recounting a conversation she had with her seven-year-old nephew Robert last week. The nephew posed to my friend his dilemma: "I found this toy and I want to keep it." The exchange between aunt and nephew proceeded: "Do you know whose it is?" "Yes, it's my best friend's." "Then you should return it to him." "But I didn't take it; he lost it." "Yes, but you know it is his; if you keep his property, that's stealing." "But I didn't steal it." "I know, but you are keeping it and it is not yours." "But it's small and he doesn't like it. He won't miss it."

Robert wasn't asking these questions because he had not thought about the seventh commandment. On the contrary, he had. Similarly, he realized that his aunt's interpretation of the seventh commandment was probably correct, but he still wanted to talk about what he considered were reasonable circumstances. The bottom line was: good fortune fell into his lap and now he had to give it up to a person who was not interested in it. Who would miss it? he wanted to know. Still, he knew that behind his questions lurked the seventh commandment. He knew that. That's why he had so many questions; he had the barest hope that maybe one question would place this new-found toy outside the concern of this commandment.

We know from any experience with children, that other than the ubiquitous and incessant "why?" question, the most common question that children have concerns fairness: Why does Sally get to stay up? Why can't I have the bigger room? Why does Johnny always get what he wants? These are not questions of simple jealousy and envy. Rather, these are questions in which children are trying to figure out what constitutes fairness. Fortunately for Robert he is still asking those questions.

Unfortunately, for many of us, the habit of asking questions about fairness has come to an end. Like Robert's, our adult world has the same occasional good "fortune": an underestimated income tax filing statement, the more-than-correct change dispensed by the machine, the wrongly added (in my favor!) restaurant check. But unlike him, we don't discuss with any nearby aunt what we have done or will do with the new fortune. In typical American fashion, we settle our concerns about fairness privately.

Our disinclination to ask questions about justice is not restricted to these petty fortunes. We also stop asking the bigger questions that underlie so many children's questions. Imagine, for instance, taking our daughter to the hospital. We see another parent and her child standing outside the hospital with the same ailment. Our daughter might ask the child's typical question, "Why isn't that girl with the same problem coming into the hospital, too?" We usually offer her the standard answer, talking about health insurance or HMOs or something like that. We know that our daughter does not seem terribly convinced of the answer, but we assure her that when she grows up she will understand.

We could share with her, however, our own adult questions, the questions that could arise specifically from our child's question. We could turn to our daughter and say, "Honey, you know I often ask myself the same question: I ask, how come we still don't have sufficient health care for all of our people? I too am troubled by that little girl, but I am also troubled that one-third of our country is just like that little girl, unable to get decent health care. I'm glad you asked that question and I hope you keep asking questions like that and that you start trying to find the answers to them." But we rarely talk like that, because we have stopped asking ourselves those questions about justice and property and wealth and rights.

We stop asking a lot of questions that deal with property and rights. We see a homeless person on the streets. Our child asks us, "why is that person living like that?" We give the standard answer about individual choices and we know that our child does not buy our answer. We could share with our child, however, a very adult question like, "You know, I have wanted to know the answer to that same question, because for the past twenty years I have seen more and more homeless persons on the streets and I can't understand it." But we don't. We have stopped asking those questions.

At some point in our moral formation we stopped asking the big questions about why some people have a lot more than others and why so many have so little. Perhaps we simply stopped being curious about who owns what and why. Perhaps we got frustrated. Perhaps we just fit into the American syndrome of believing in that odd phrase "to each his own." In any event, we stopped asking the questions.

The curious thing is that since it's inception the seventh commandment generated a host of questions. Think of the books of Deuteronomy or Numbers or Judges. Or think of Amos or Jeremiah. Our forbearers found it to be the commandment that generated the most questions. Likewise, our children ask unending but probing questions about it. So how is it that the questions we could ask are the questions that only children ask?

This has been my question in writing this essay. Rather than answer it, I simply highlight how important it is that we listen to the questions of children. From their voices, I think, we hear the questions that indeed we could really articulate. So, I conclude with a story that the late Dr. Martin Luther King, Jr., tells about a question his daughter asked.

> The family often used to ride with me to the Atlanta airport, and on our way, we always passed Funtown, a sort of miniature Disneyland with mechanical rides and that sort of thing. Yolanda would inevitably say, "I want to go to Funtown," and I would always evade a direct reply. I really didn't know how to explain to her why she couldn't go. Then one day at home, she ran downstairs exclaiming that a TV commercial was urging people to come to Funtown. Then my wife and I had to sit down with her between us and try to explain it. I have won some applause as a speaker, but my tongue

twisted and my speech stammered seeking to explain to my six-year-old daughter why the public invitation didn't include her and others like her. One of the most painful experiences I have ever faced was to see her tears when I told her that Funtown was closed to colored children, for I realized that at the moment the first dark cloud of inferiority had floated into her little mental sky, that at that moment her personality had begun to warp with the first unconscious bitterness toward white people. It was the first time that prejudice based upon skin color had been explained to her. But it was of paramount importance to me that she not grow up bitter" [*A Testament of Hope: The Essential Writings of Martin Luther King, Jr.* (p. 342)].

Yolanda was robbed of the innocence of childhood by a society that did not ask the questions about fairness that she asked. But she did. And, fortunately her father didn't like the standard answer that he gave. Instead, he heard her question, recognized its legitimacy, and sought a way of answering it, satisfactorily. Like Dr. King, we need to become attuned again to the questions of children, for no other reason, than to get into the habit of expressing, once again, our own.

CHAPTER EIGHT

The Eighth Commandment

"You shall not bear false witness against your neighbor" (Ex 20:16).

Don't kill, commit adultery, steal, or lie—the fifth, sixth, seventh, and eighth commandments—that's basically how I understood them and I am sure that's how many readers understood them. But throughout these essays we have seen that behind every "don't" is a "do." Thus, the foundations of each of the four commandments are respectively: respect life and the body; promote justice and the truth. Regarding the eighth commandment in particular, the failure to promote truth leads to false witnessing against the neighbor; indeed, every false witness occurs because the witness does not want the neighbor's truth to be heard. To promote truth, then, we need to create space where truth can be told.

THE NEED FOR SPACE WHERE TRUTH CAN BE TOLD

In a powerful movie based on Brian Moore's futuristic novel *Catholics,* Trevor Howard plays an abbot whose abbey refuses to conform to the progressive standards of a new Vatican III Council. A very modern Vatican representative arrives to investigate but finds the abbot a prudential and orthodox superior. The investigator learns, however, that the abbot is terrified of praying. Never sensing the presence of

God, he never is able to finish the Our Father. "Why didn't you tell anyone?" asks the incredulous investigator. "Because I am too ashamed. Who would I tell? One of the men who relies on me, who looks up to me? You are the only priest I have seen in years who is not a subject." But the investigator had no advice and left unable to render him any assistance. The stunning movie ends with the troubled abbot alone, terrified, on his knees, uttering, "Our Father, who art . . ."

I know how he felt. After four years of teaching at Fordham, I came to teach at Weston. After my first month here, my dad died suddenly of a heart attack at the age of sixty-two. Afterward, as I prayed I encountered nothing but darkness and an abyss. It was very painful. I told no one. Later, my superior asked me how things were going in light of my dad's death. I told him that every night I just fell off asleep begging God for some sense of well-being or, at least, to lift the darkness. "How long has this been going on?" "For ten months." "Why didn't you tell anyone?" "I'm a priest teaching at a seminary. I was too embarrassed that I don't have greater faith."

My superior provided me with a way to relate my experience. By speaking with him I learned that I was not suffering from a lack of faith. Through him, I realized that I believed deeply; my prayer, however, was desolate. By talking through my experience, I could find a more accurate understanding of the truth, but I could never have found it, if he hadn't provided me the space to speak.

A VERY REAL NEED

Like pastors and superiors, spiritual directors know that they must not only listen, respond, and remember, but also try to make sure that people can speak about whatever is going on in their lives as they stand before God. That's not easy. Many people are unable to bring to the surface some of their felt experiences. They may believe, as I did, that their experiences are too unique, inappropriate, or unorthodox. Unless they are offered space where they can speak truly, they remain trapped by their own, often inhibiting, thoughts. To create an atmosphere of trust, to help people talk truthfully about their experiences, and to let them believe what they experience bears mentioning constitutes, I think, the fundamental concern of the eighth commandment.

Any confessor knows this. The sacrament of reconciliation requires the priest to provide a forum where penitents can speak what they have long kept in silence. He knows how careful he must be to let them find a way of saying what they have long dreaded to confess. If penitents, spiritual directees, and those in ministry need help to utter the truth, can we not assume that we each need that help?

OUR CULTURE DOES NOT INVITE PEOPLE TO TRUTH TELLING

Intolerance and ridicule frequently inhibit honesty. Consider, for instance, the landmark "don't ask, don't tell" compromise for homosexuals in the armed forces. No one will tolerate homosexuals' self-disclosures. Or, remember when President Carter acknowledged that he lusted in his heart after other women; the talk shows had a field day with that honest remark.

Though both tendencies inhibit us from telling truthfully our own experiences, three other obstacles are much more problematic: litigiousness, self-deception about our private lives, and lack of leadership. First, we are a people governed more by law than by custom or morals. As the most litigious society that has ever existed, we are often inhibited from expressing our concerns. For example, how many physicians, nurses and staff, or drivers, bikers, and pedestrians, or producers, distributors, and sellers have failed to apologize for harm caused because they were advised against acknowledging any fault in light of possible litigation? Or consider how the last decade taught us the need to respect boundaries and power inequities. These lessons were formulated and brokered through the courts. But, how well do people today in businesses, services, and education understand these issues as moral? Do they know what is right or wrong as opposed to what is legal or illegal? Was there a context in which to consider the ethical while lawyers and judges arbitrated social interactions?

When our nation learned that President Clinton misled us for months regarding his extramarital affair with Monica Lewinsky, we wondered: Why didn't the President tell us the truth in the first place? Because he was under investigation. Why did he tell us the truth, finally? Many would say, to avoid impeachment. Prosecution inhibited the truth; later, it forced the truth; but it never created a space to simply speak the whole truth.

Another obstacle is the tattered cloak of privacy. Think, for instance, of the many, many politicians who believed that their private activities would not affect their public judgment. That belief has done more harm to more important leaders than any other categorical type of misjudgment. But the public too is conflicted about the right to privacy: on the one hand it acts as though every public figure is entitled to privacy; on the other hand, it is unable to respect or uphold that right. The public becomes as self-deceptive as are the politicians. Claiming to surrender any interest in politicians' off-hours activities, the public is more familiar with one young woman's dress than with political affairs in Africa, Russia, or Asia.

If we would drop our conflicted and obsessive relationship about privacy and instead learn more about tolerance, human failure, the real possibility of broken promises . . . if we learned to allow others to speak, acknowledge, opine, or even, if necessary, confess and repent, we could become a society promoting truthfulness. Are we today? Do we see any indicators of our society promoting truthfulness?

This leads to a third obstacle: we have no credible leadership urging us to promote the truth.

WHAT OF OUR CHURCH?

The church, too, needs to promote a space where its members can talk truthfully to one another. Consider, as one example, the experience of moral theologians today. Our greatest problem, I think, is that seminary teachers are subject to more and more scrutiny by more and more bishops. Talented moral theologians— trained, interested, and dedicated to teaching in seminaries—are

fleeing to the American university system where they can be protected by academic freedom. Barring an honest, extended, tolerant,
and respectful discussion among bishops and theologians, many
believe that the seminary is becoming less and less a place for theological investigation or for speaking about practical matters of conscience. What does this say about a church that needs to train well
the next generation of people called to ministry? What does it say
about a church that was the "next generation" called to ministry?
What does it say about a church founded by apostles who collectively tried to discern the truth about who Jesus of Nazareth was?

On the other hand, throughout the United States many parishes
thrive precisely because they witness to the truth as they discern it
in their lives. Though some parishes and their members are still
inhibited by intolerant organizations and/or fearful leadership, many
other parishes promote a tolerant exchange of ideas: parish members discuss candidly financial matters; through twelve-step programs, people acknowledge the limitedness of their lives; parish
councils allow pastors and members to grapple with a variety of
concrete concerns; youth groups provide a context for youth leadership on a parish level; and, adult study groups allow for the laity and
their leaders to become theologically informed and articulate. These
are signs and models for hope, as Charles Morris notes in his
American Catholic.

Aside from local parishes, the national Catholic leadership project
known as the Catholic Common Ground Initiative is, by promoting
tolerant communication, another beacon of hope. When the late
Cardinal Joseph Bernardin first inaugurated that project I was personally challenged by it. I recognized that I did not always consider-
ately represent other theologians, especially those with whom I
disagreed (the very issue of the eighth commandment). In light of
the project statement, I acknowledged that I was wrong and pledged
to my students that I would more faithfully represent other theologians' points of view. I learned from him and those in the project
what it meant to promote the eighth commandment: not to misrep-
resent others, but rather to listen and learn from one another and to
seek collectively, but not relatively, to express the truth correctly.

We need to recognize the challenge today to speak what we believe. We need to recognize the call for clear leadership to guide all of us in the pursuit of truth. We need to invite one another to speak the truth as we understand it, so that in a loving and respectful context we may together discover and articulate the truth as it really is. That's not an ideal; it is a command.

CHAPTER NINE

The Ninth Commandment

*"Neither shall you covet your
neighbor's wife" (Dt 5:21).*

The descent from the very first commandment to the last
two is a constant one: from the sovereignty of God to
human action and finally to our deepest desires as humans.
Having considered the commandments on respecting God
and parents, the commandments turn to four main areas of
life (life, the body, property, and one's reputation); they conclude with our internal desires, especially regarding our spouse
and, then, our neighbors' property. Together they command us
to keep our desires well-ordered. The Reformers recognized
this distinctive end to the commandments, this internal end.
Both Martin Luther and John Calvin described the commandments on covetousness as referring to our deepest
desires.

DISCERNING OUR DEEPEST DESIRES

Any preacher can capture her or his congregation by simply
asking the people to reflect on their deepest desires. Try it:
invite the community to consider what they hope for, pray for,
yearn for. Their eyes convey immediately that they have dared
to enter that reflective realm where emotions are allowed to
engage their most substantive longings. Encourage your congregation to consider the horizon of their expectations: letting

themselves see what they so often unconsciously expect. Is it marriage and family? Is it friends or a job? Is it satisfaction in the family, the workplace, or oneself? Does the listener have cancer and is she expecting to face it boldly with her friends, family, and resourceful physicians?

In any congregation of four hundred and three persons, there are four hundred and three persons with deep desires. Deep desires frame our lives: they make us happy, sad, fretful, self-pitying, elated, engaging, frustrated, secure, dependent, and a host of other states of being. Our deepest desires are where we live, but rarely we touch, acknowledge, or reflect on them. Thus, a congregation invited to reflect on these deep desires is one that usually becomes very engaged by the exercise.

We rarely articulate or express deep desires. Why? Because our wishes are not simple: we cannot say, "Oh, this is all I wish for!" "If I had this, I would be forever satisfied!" Certainly, we may occasionally say these things, but we don't mean them. Our deep desires are wonderfully complex, tending in a variety of directions, wanting satisfaction in a myriad of ways. Given all these deep desires, how do we catch a glimpse of them, beyond the preacher's invitation to consider them on a Sunday morning?

Recently I asked a congregation to consider the last time they were disappointed, really disappointed. Was it their children or community members arguing, was it someone not seeing through a resolution they promised to keep, was it an agreed expectation never met? Whatever that disappointment was, it was a disappointment of one of those deep desires.

When our expectations are contradicted, we become disappointed. We are disappointed precisely when our expectations are replaced by the regrettably unexpected: the bickering at an anniversary party, the arguing at a birthday celebration, the rejection by a friend. As bleak as these disappointments are, they are windows to our deepest desires. In them we can see what our hopes and wishes actually are. By our disappointments we get a sense of how deep and heartfelt our desires actually are.

Disappointment is not the only marker that lets us know about our deepest desires. They play out in our conscious and unconscious lives all the time. For instance, we can see something that makes us smile: a baby, a couple in love, a beautiful flower. Our smile lets us know that we have just seen something that fits in with our deepest desires. In a similar way, when we are suddenly shocked, that jarring sensation lets us know just how connected we are to something or to someone. Unfortunately, often, we don't know about the importance of that connection until it is abruptly severed. There, in the shock of loss, the words of a song make striking sense: "You don't know what you've got 'til its gone." Loss awakens us to our deepest desires, too.

We become aware of our deepest desires, then, through a variety of sudden emotional states, whether they are enjoyable ones that pleasantly stir us—like a smile, a touch, or a greeting—or unpleasant ones that startle us. Awakened we recognize something about our deep desires: these are the images of the kingdom of God that we carry inside of us; they represent our image of the kingdom. Though it may not be terribly focused, that image deals with families and friends, strangers and neighbors, previous and future generations. The kingdom of God lives in our expectations for the variety of complex relationships that we enjoy. The kingdom, then, is about our moral universe where we wish one another well. In that moral universe we believe that God abides with us and protects us. As Christians we have a deeply abiding and viscerally felt image of the kingdom of God that we carry in our hearts.

ORDERING OUR LOVES

Our desires are, then, about those whom we love. In fact, if we were to talk about moral theology or ethics, as Saint Augustine once did, we would call it an ordering of loves. The ethical enterprise is about putting our loves in order. In this way we achieve our deepest desires. Our ordered loves help us to realize them.

For this reason the ninth commandment reminds us that we ought to put no other person in the way of our ordered loves. No other person ought to be the cause of our jeopardizing those loves and our deepest desires. The ninth commandment warns us against the possibility of throwing the entire complexity of our relationships aside by another relationship. We know this possibility to be true. Husbands or wives who pursue another's spouse harm not only themselves and the other spouses, but the children, parents, and friends involved in those marriages. The damage from adultery is far more extensive than what is felt by the two or three persons involved. But the ninth commandment concerns not only married persons. Single people, clergy, and vowed religious know that it is possible to endanger so many of our relationships by the emotional pursuit of another relationship that contradicts the commitments we presently enjoy. We know how certain personal entanglements can compromise us and our relationships and we know that so many persons can be adversely affected by such entanglements.

A CALL TO ATTENTIVENESS

The commandment calls us to be attentive, to avoid not only dangerous liaisons, but even the possibility of such relationships. It calls us to be alert to the possibility of undoing our deepest desires and charges us to focus our deepest desires on those to whom we are *already committed*. It reminds us to consider what is at stake when we begin lusting after another. Thus, it reminds us to be more mindful of our deepest desires.

The ninth commandment offers us guidance at the more unconscious or semi-conscious levels of our existence. It enters into that world where we fantasize, muse, and daydream. It asks us to consider the longings, yearnings, and unspoken hopes that fleetingly yet deeply and often pass through our minds and hearts. It invites us to see that these attractive images affect our psyches, the very fabric of our existence. It invites us to consider our most visceral desires and hopes and to be attentive to our fantasies. Do our fantasies lead us to deepening and ordering our loves? Do we muse about those whom we love, to whom we are committed, for whom we live?

Or do we engage fantasies that mislead us? Do we yearn for relationships that do nothing to support the loves we now enjoy, but instead unsettle and threaten the very foundations upon which our loves are based? Are our daydreams, playful thoughts, and wishing moments sustaining and nourishing our loves or are they escape hatches leading us into realms that are not a part of our desires?

The ninth commandment is an invasive one. It looks not at our external actions, but our inner thoughts, aspirations, and yearnings. It slaps us out of our dozing and indulgent fantasies by warning us against coveting. And yet, in its intrusiveness, the commandment is not a prohibition of pleasure, delight, or enjoyment. On the contrary, it is given for our own good. In recognizing how difficult it is for us to access our deepest desires, the commandment invites us to more consciously call to mind the variety of ways we love. Then it leads us to appreciate our longings, fantasies, and musings as occasions for sustaining the relationships that make us who we are.

The ninth commandment recognizes, then, our humanity. Candidly it engages us where we engage others, in our hearts and our minds. It invites us to see what we so often are unaware of: that everything and everyone we hold to dearly, ought to be dearly held.

CHAPTER TEN

The Tenth Commandment

"Neither shall you desire your neighbor's house, or field, or male or female slave, or ox, or donkey, or anything that belongs to your neighbor" (Dt 5:21).

COVETING HOUSES

When I was a boy in Brooklyn I wanted to be a farmer. My parents reminded me often that I had never seen a farm in Brooklyn. Eventually they talked me out of the farming aspiration (God knows where it came from). For a few years after that I wanted to be an architect, but I also gave up that dream. By then I wanted to and finally did become a priest. Occasionally I wonder what it would have been like to be either a farmer or an architect. While those decisions seem to be in the distant past, I am occasionally reminded of them because there's nothing I covet more than a beautifully constructed home. I don't covet anyone's livestock or cornfields, but a well-planned mansion is something else.

Right now, I am living at John Carroll University in Cleveland where I am a visiting professor of moral theology for the semester. When I go running in the morning I pass extraordinarily beautiful homes on Fairmount, North Park, and South Park. I would love to own one of those homes. Passing by them I fantasize what it would be like to have this one or that one.

The more I think about my wish to have one, the more disappointed I am that I don't own one. Curiously, I compound my disappointment and become doubly miserable: miserable about what I don't have and miserable that I don't have it.

WHAT DO WE COVET?

Coveting is such an ordinary disposition that we do not recognize how frequently we do covet until we really stop and think about it. When I mentioned to a colleague here, for instance, that I coveted a house on Fairmount, he said he knew exactly which one! I am sure that there are many readers who long for a particular house out there and experience the same double misery when they consider it. Or someone who travels and pines for a particular location or property and who also experiences the double misery. "Phew," we say to ourselves, "When will I be there?" Then we get the double whammy: "What I want, I don't have; I'm not there."

Some of us covet success more than property. We would like the parish in such and such a neighborhood; we would like to be selected for this particular board or committee; we would like to win a particular recognition.

Though we may not be aware of everything we covet, we can be sure that there are several things in life that we covet. Sometimes it is good to list what we really covet if only to find out what it is we would like to have. Bringing what we covet to the surface of our own consciousness keeps us from being blind to the subtle messages that influence many of our ordinary decisions. For what we covet usually reminds us of where our dissatisfactions really are.

AN INVITATION TO FRUSTRATION OR TO GRATITUDE

I think of coveting as arising from the void of dissatisfaction. I say this because I have come to realize that the opposite of coveting is a grateful satisfaction with one's lot. Such satisfaction does not come easily for me or for many of us.

When I was a graduate student in Rome, I had a spiritual director who believed (probably rightly) that I had high expectations about, well, everything. He was a young British priest from the diocese of London and in every one of my sessions with him, he'd respond to at least one insight of mine with the phrase, "that sounds like an expectation." Often he was annoying, but always he was right. I wanted everything always to go perfectly. I lived in a world of great expectations about everything so I was always disappointed. As a result, my anticipations of the future were so emphatically destined to miss the mark that I was often unsettled and unrequited.

My director wanted me to get to a more realistic frame of reference where I could learn what the feeling of satisfaction actually was. To get there I first had to learn the "attitude of gratitude." What I learned from him, many learn from twelve-step programs. Members of these programs recognize the importance of gratitude for living with compulsions for alcohol, food, sex, and so on. In order to curb their compulsions, these members understand the significance of acknowledging what they already have and enjoy. Gratitude reminds them that their lot is a pretty good one.

In the Jesuit community in Cambridge where I normally live, we have a practice of gratitude. During every dinner, after the main course and before coffee, we read a brief passage of Scripture and then invite everyone present, guests included, to thank God for whatever we are grateful for. It has had a wonderful impact on each of us, helping us to see really how good our lives are. This daily practice of gratitude has made us a better community.

Expressing gratitude is an effective act. If we merely think about gratitude, we may not experience how fortunate we really are. In our mind we may be somewhat inclined to think that our own predicament is satisfactory, but not until we actually state our gratitude do we also judge and express our situation as a fortunate one. Then, and only then, do we achieve a sense of well-being about how good things are.

For this reason, twelve-step programs encourage their members to express the attitude of gratitude. Without the expression, there is a longing for something else.

SATISFACTION

An enduring attitude of gratitude leads to a state of satisfaction. Sometimes, I think, we believe that satisfaction is a terribly boring disposition. We think of satisfaction as some sort of disincentive to hope or to dream: If Dr. Martin Luther King were satisfied, where would our country be today? We think of satisfaction as inhibiting any creative energy or imaginative impulses: If God were satisfied, we think, God would never have created the world.

Any satisfaction that inhibits possible human flourishment is not, by definition, a virtue. But there is a satisfaction that comes from grateful, dynamic people. Pastors on the way to greatness, for instance, are always thanking their lucky stars. They don't covet what another pastor has; rather they see what they already have, are grateful for it, draw energy from their sense of satisfaction, and move ahead. They don't want or pine for what another has: houses, success, location. Rather they see their life as a positive journey that continues to play itself out.

Any person who has lived in poverty knows this type of satisfaction. They know that the act of coveting just leads to more frustration. They know that their satisfaction may not be about the quality of safety on their streets or the roof over their heads. But they know that where things go right, where people are responsible, and where love is strong, that they are grateful. Thus, like Dr. Martin Luther King, they do not buy that false satisfaction that says "you should wait." They know they need to assert their rights, but they also know that if they covet, they will be diverted from their agenda. Instead, satisfied with the people they are and the people with whom they work, they move ahead knowing that only in that way will their journey to greater justice be a positive one.

A PERFECT CONCLUSION

The tenth commandment is a perfect complement to the first one. The first one reminds us that God is God, that God delivers and protects us, and that in gratitude we should place no false gods before us. Likewise, the last commandment reminds us that we have much to be grateful for and that we should not pine after what is not ours; it warns us against false idols. It invites us to see where we are, to reflect on our lot as more gift than achievement, and to have hope in the future, accepting it as an opportunity for moving dynamically forward with a liberating sense of satisfaction with how well life's journey is going.

The tenth commandment is like all the other commands from God, a command leading us to our happiness. It is a gift that warns us against a double misery and offers instead a double happiness: a happiness with our present lot and a calm expectation for our future.

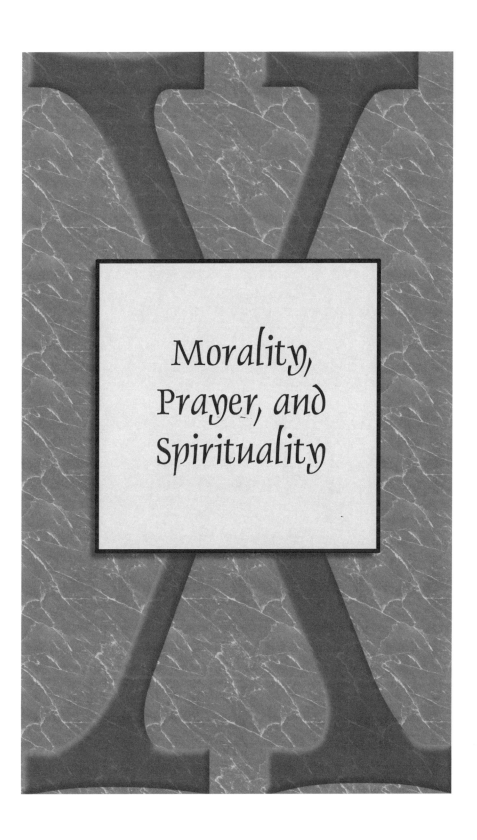

Morality, Prayer, and Spirituality

CHAPTER ELEVEN

Prayer and the Moral Life

Now that we have meditated on each of the Ten Commandments, I want to recall a story that I told in my last book, *Virtues for Ordinary Christians*. During my years of study at the Gregorian University in Rome, I spent summers in either Germany or Austria studying part-time and working in a parish part-time. One summer when I was living in Munich, I decided to go to Dachau. I specifically wanted to pray there and had heard that I could pray next to the camp at a convent chapel maintained by a group of women religious. One of the Jesuits in the community where I lived was chaplain to the sisters and told me that I could pray there, even on Mondays when the camp and its museum were closed. So I set out one cloudy Monday to pray at Dachau.

PRAYING AT DACHAU

Forgoing a bus that could have taken me directly from the train station, I walked about three or four miles. As I walked, I became angrier and angrier. All I saw were nice, suburban houses with manicured lawns—no trace of the tragedy of Dachau. I started asking myself, How could anyone after 1945 live in a city called Dachau? What type of people would not mind having as a mailing address the name of a place notorious for persecution? I thought, if ghosts exist, they would haunt this town. As I walked, seeing the cinder-blocked camp ahead of me, I wondered how anyone could claim seriously not to have known about the killings. As I drew closer, the skies were dark. Off to the side of the main street that led to the camp, I saw a new white, Alpine-looking church. I wondered, Who were these people who could claim that God was here in this place where they and their forebears conspired to kill so many Jews, gypsies, homosexuals, and others?

I was surprised by the length of the camp as I walked the whole way to the rear of it and rang the bell of the convent where I had come to pray. A voice in German told me that the convent was closed. I responded that I was not a tourist; that I came only to pray. "We're closed," the German sister repeated. "I'm a Jesuit and your chaplain told me that I could pray here." "We're closed." "Can't I pray?" "We're closed; it's Monday."

I had come to Dachau to pray, but was not allowed to. I began my trek back, even angrier than before. The skies were darker and my spirits were filled with rage. I again passed by the new white church just outside the camp; for a moment I thought I might pray there but I quickly decided that I did not come to pray in the church where conspirers pray; I came to pray where the persecuted died. I decided not to pray there in that white church.

Yet I had come to Dachau to pray and here was a place of opportunity. Surely I shouldn't avoid the very point of my journey. So I crossed the road and entered the white church. I looked up at the altar and there I saw it. Suspended over the altar was an enormous corpus of the suffering Christ, crucified not to wood but to the very barbed wire that the people of this town had once made. There was the suffering Christ, the Jew, and his cross had been fashioned by the Catholics of this town. They knew their guilt. And with as much speed as it took for me to see the barbed wire, I knew my guilt as well.

I sat down stunned. For one hour I sat overthrown by my own guilt, wickedness, and sinfulness—awash in it. Yet, I did not feel any worry. Instead, I felt light. I felt that somehow Christ wanted me to know myself—my pettiness, my selfishness, my seething judgment—but would not let me be shattered by the knowledge. I was overcome by my badness and yet Christ's strength, light, and love would not let me be lost. I felt oddly confident, extraordinarily vulnerable, yet confident.

After an hour or so, I prayed for all the people my selfishness had harmed. I begged their forgiveness and I thanked God for this revelation of myself and of God's tenderness. I left the church. Outside, as I looked up, the skies were beautifully blue with wisps of clouds across the horizon. A little boy, passing by on his tricycle, saw me and uttered the wonderful Bavarian greeting, "Grüss Gott!" ("God's greetings!"). I sat down on the curb and cried. My prayer that day was truly blessed.

Prayer and morality are, in some people's minds, strange bedfellows. With the exception of James Keating's articles in CHURCH and Mark O'Keefe's *Becoming Good, Becoming Holy*, moral theologians rarely write about prayer and writers on prayer rarely write about morality. Nevertheless, prayer and the moral life are indispensable for one another. Here, then I want to explore three key notions of prayer that are important for the moral life.

AN ENCOUNTER WITH GOD

First, prayer is a meeting, an encounter with God. Above all, prayer is a rendezvous with the Other as Other. Nothing is more central. That needs to be said, in part because the effect of prayer is often that we know more about ourselves. Even though prayer is an encounter with God, we actually learn more about ourselves than about God. Prayer would be simply a lesson in self-knowledge if we did not realize, however, that in prayer we know ourselves "as we are known." That is, in prayer God lets us know ourselves as God knows us. Just as God broke through my shell of anger and revealed to me my true self, so much of our encounter with God is God's revelation of ourselves to us.

Likewise, in that prayer I was able to see how the people of Dachau saw themselves in God's eyes. Their shame and guilt was there before them every time they assembled together in prayer. They knew concretely what their sin was as they saw the very barbed wire that they had fashioned to harness and kill their own neighbors. And they let their prayer be public; the story of their sin and Christ's redemption was there not only for them to see, but for me and all visitors as well. The story of God's revelation of themselves to them became my own.

Certainly real prayer is an encounter with God who reveals to us our own selves as well as God's self. But that revelation, like God's touching love, is ineffable. None of us dare say what God is like, except that God is love. We walk away from prayer knowing that we have met God, but we do not say anything more about God. Rather than talk about God, we participate like Moses in a holy silence, not trying to describe the One who makes us.

In that encounter we can know ourselves. This indeed is the prayer of the "daily examination" of self that Saint Ignatius left us, the prayer by which we ask God for light, that we may see how God moves us and how we respond. Prayer is disclosure of One who loves and reveals to us who, in turn, see where we have been led and where we have chosen to go.

A MOVEMENT OR FEELING

The second dimension of prayer is movement or feeling. No feelings, no prayer. Dryness is the way those who pray describe the "absence" of God. The absence of feelings is a clear sign of desolation. Feelings are constitutive of prayer. By prayer we feel that we are moved.

My early years in the Society of Jesus I sometimes describe pejoratively as "Irish Gothic." I sensed several of the province's spiritual gurus telling me, "Be Still and know that I am God." Their spirituality and prayer was stark. Mine wasn't. They were always telling me that my prayer was too "busy," filled with, what they called, "distractions." But every time I tried to move away from the distraction, my prayer got drier. It was not until years later that I was fortunate enough to be at the altar during Mass at the Basilica of Loyola. As we approached the consecration, I could see everyone's eyes fixed on the host, while mine were all over the basilica. From the host, to the cup, to the cupola where seven virtues lined the rim, my eyes took in the church's expanse. I realized then that my spirituality was closer to my preferred religious architecture, baroque. Gothic may have dominated my province back home, but in my life, the wildly imaginative and terribly busy and distracting baroque God animated me.

While I love an eight-day retreat, I can also say, not surprisingly, that I pray best during a morning run. I feel so close to God when I run that I cannot but call it prayer. God is with me in a particular way and as God's movements come and go, I know tangibly that I am with God. It's where God leads me.

I share these rather unorthodox images in part that we may encourage one another to let God work in our lives not as we think God should, but rather as God does. God moves us in different places and different ways, but where we feel the hand of God, we must let it touch, probe, lead. We must let God communicate God's self to us. Prayer is where we are moved to freedom. If we straitjacket prayer, we will never be freed.

GOD'S PROVIDENTIAL PRESENCE

Finally, prayer is God's providential presence. In prayer God leads us to see that somehow we can hope because God is God. In my shame, guilt, and repentance at Dachau, God led me to see my wickedness but also God's care and tenderness. There in the city where Jews, gypsies, and homosexuals were killed by righteous Christians, I saw my own hating self. There, too, I experienced the reassuring presence of God, who extended himself from the cross.

I was led that day in Dachau. God left me to my own righteousness and great anger, only to lead me to that white church and that barbed wired fence, and then to utter those words of greeting to me. God reminded me that God is God.

Now, years later, as I remember that day, I realize that God was teaching me why the Ten Commandments begin with the first one. For learning that God is God is the experience of prayer. Without that lesson, I will never know myself or my neighbor, whom I have never loved enough or my God who loves us all.

CHAPTER TWELVE

Rooting Morality in Spirituality

When I was a graduate student at the Gregorian University in Rome, Father Klaus Demmer asked us: As a Christian if you meet a person in need on the street, do you respond to her because you see her in need or because you see Christ in need? Later the professor said, "Though there are many today who preach that Christians respond to the person in need because they see Christ in the person, I think there is another side to the Christian tradition that calls us to respond simply to the neighbor in need. If later in prayer, we are given the grace by God to see that the neighbor in need was Christ, so be it. But let God show us that, and let that revelation be after we have responded to the neighbor."

Demmer was concerned about an overly spiritualized view of morality where we look for Christ and don't see the particular person before us. If everyone in need is Christ, how do we differentiate their needs from one another? If we are looking for Christ, we can, with our own expectations of who Christ is, overlook our neighbor because her needs don't conform to what we believe are Christ's needs. Our image of Christ might prevent us from seeing who stands before us.

Demmer pointed us to key insights from the Christian tradition. The Samaritan in Luke's parable, for instance, is a good person simply responding to another in need, concerned not with who the person was, but rather that he was injured and in need of help. Likewise, in Matthew 25, we find the well-known judgment scene where the goats and sheep are separated. Jesus invites the sheep into the kingdom, "I was hungry and you fed me, naked and you clothed me. . . ." They ask, "but when did we see you hungry . . . ?" Jesus answers that it was when they fed the hungry. They were not looking to feed a hungry Christ; rather they saw a hungry person and fed her. Only at the last judgment in the story does Jesus reveal to them who the hungry person was. They did not see Christ in whom they served; but Christ revealed to them that it was he whom they ultimately served when they reached out to others.

This same insight is caught later in many stories that surround our saints. When Saint Martin of Tours gives his cloak to a man in need, it is later revealed to him that the man was Christ. While not denying that some Christians claim to respond to the need of others because they see Christ, others like Demmer prefer to see that the Christians' call is to see the neighbor specifically.

IS THAT ALL THERE IS?

Is being a Christian simply loving my neighbor as he or she is? To answer, let me ask another question: For the Christian, what is the most important moral commandment? Is it simply to love your neighbor as yourself? Is that adequate? Or, do we need to say first that it is to love the Lord your God with your whole heart, your whole mind, your whole body, and your whole soul? Does the command to love God mean anything specifically, or do we say that to love God is simply to love your neighbor?

I believe certainly that we should love our neighbor in the concrete, as she is, with her particular set of needs. But I also believe that the reason why I am compassionate, why I am responsive, and why I am even able to see the person in need is because God has placed within me the ability to see, to respond, to be compassionate. I do not believe that I can be charitable without the grace of God. Certainly I am called to be like the Good Samaritan; but I am able to be like him only through God's grace. If I am at all responsive to a person, any person, it is because Christ is working within me, calling me to realize the talents within me.

Moral theology, then, begins not with our response, but with God's initiative. The call to the moral life is not a matter of our making a decision to be nice, moral, thoughtful, or even holy. It is not founded on our decision; rather, it begins with God's. God called us and the agenda that we need to assert is not one founded by and through humans but by God. God calls us to see our neighbor in need and God gives us the grace to respond.

We too often think that the decision to be moral comes first from ourselves. But just as God gave the Ten Commandments to Moses at Mount Sinai and just as Jesus gave his listeners the Beatitudes in the Sermon on the Mount, so God calls us to the moral life and gives us the ability to respond. It is true that we decide, but only because God first decided and because God made our decision possible. We forget this. But the moral life is not only God's initiative, it is God's empowerment. Not only does God invite us to be moral, but God works within us through grace so that we can be moral.

We can only understand the call to love my neighbor as myself (note here, we are to love both!), when we first understand the call to love God with my whole self. That is, the moral life is only understood when we understand that before we claim to love our neighbor, God claims us. God tells us concretely "I am the Lord your God."

When God claims us, God at once commands us to love God in return. For there is no other way for us to love God, but to love our neighbor as ourselves. We are certainly to love our neighbor as uniquely as we are to love ourselves. But the command is rooted in the command to love God, the foundation of the moral life. The command to love God then is not simply the command to love our neighbor. It is the invitation to acknowledge that the first interest in us and in our neighbor originated not from us, but from our Maker, Redeemer, and Sanctifier. The entire enterprise about being moral rests on God's concern for us.

WE NEED A MORALITY
BASED ON A SPIRITUALITY

Our entire morality is based on a spirituality. Over the last thirty years, moral theology has undergone an enormous change in this direction. Consider, for example, the penitential rite. Before Vatican II we confessed that we sinned "in thought, word, and deed." After the Council we added "that I have sinned . . . in what I have done and in what I have failed to do." This shift in thinking of sin as not only what we have done but also as what we have failed to do is significant.

For centuries, moral theologians wrote about sin in terms of actions—what a person did. They rarely wrote about the need to confess conduct which we did not engage. This is not to say that people never confessed failing to be an "understanding spouse" or a "grateful child." But those ideas came from the penitent's heart or from the gentle prodding of the confessor, not from the moral theologian. For centuries moral theologians basically measured what was sinful and what was not. And they considered sin as what one did or thought about doing. The moral theologian considered what a person should avoid, not what one should pursue.

That singular concern with sinful deeds came under criticism at Vatican II. Members of the Council wrote that moral theology "should draw more fully on the teaching of the Holy Scripture and should throw light upon the exalted vocation of the faithful in Christ and their obligation to bring forth fruit in charity for the life of the world" (*Document on Priestly Formation,* 16). This simple statement meant that moral theologians needed to help others hear Christ's call to "bring forth fruit in charity." The Council taught us that to be moral was not simply avoiding sin; to be moral primarily meant answering the call of Christ.

THE MORAL LIFE AS
THE CHRISTIAN VOCATION

For this reason, after the Council moralists began scrambling to find ways to express the moral life as the "Christian vocation." Several European theologians wrote books about morality and discipleship, asking how we could follow in the footsteps of Christ. One American moral theologian, Norbert Rigali, followed the Europeans' lead, insisting that morality and spirituality needed to be better related.

He was right. Spirituality has always concerned our relationship with the Lord; morality had been relegated to "what we did." By putting them together, we could start talking about what our moral lives were like in the context of our relationship with the Lord.

If we continue to follow the direction Vatican II has set, we should examine how, concretely, we can engage in a moral theology based on a spirituality—that is, based on a positive agenda about what we do in response to God's invitation to follow in Jesus' footsteps. The beginning of that agenda, of course, is the call to acknowledge God as the divine initiator and the source of all our strength.

Goodness
and
Rightness

CHAPTER THIRTEEN

What Does Right and Wrong Have to Do with Good and Bad?

Or

If You Think an Action is Right But it Isn't and You Do It, Are You Bad?

What am I asking? Am I proposing a way out of irresponsible activity? Am I proposing some clever Jesuitical exercise so that you can deny or cover up whatever you intend to do? No. I am posing a question that presumes sincerity and rejects deceit or fraud. It's a question we can ask of anyone in any situation, anyone, that is, who sincerely tries to do the right but fails.

We can ask it of the physician who tries to make the right prognosis, but does not. Consider the teacher who does not know whether she ought to approach her student with "tough love" or support, and somehow picks the wrong approach. Consider the spouse who does not know whether to pry or to let alone the spouse who has not communicated well in days. Consider the student with a dominating roommate or the parent with the troubled child or the child with an isolated parent. These are all ordinary cases, the very kind we often encounter but more often overlook in moral reflection. Their importance is that they demonstrate how we think and judge morally in ordinary times.

Some readers may be asking, Who is to say what is wrong? That is not the question under consideration here, however.

Consider the ordinary case: a person tries to get some task right and ends up doing it wrong. The physician errs in her prognosis; instead of healing, she actually harms the patient. It is an ordinary error involving no rare disease and requiring no extraordinary knowledge. Despite the physician's effort, she still did not find what another physician might have. She made a mistake. Likewise the teacher who decides to exercise tough love might be doing the wrong thing. Even before the sparks fly, others can see that in this particular instance tough love is inappropriate. The same with the student who capitulates to the manipulative roommate when it is obvious to any observer that she should be assertive. Instead, in the name of harmony the student erroneously lets the roommate have her way. In each of these instances, the agent gets it wrong, despite efforts to get it right.

It is like those few but dreadful moments when we arrive home and our child, spouse, parent, friend, or community member greets us at the door with "She meant well," "He did it out of love," or "He really didn't mean it." Such phrases tell us that someone tried to do right, but did not. Warned, we know that disaster lies beyond the portal.

ACTING IN CONSCIENCE

The question I am asking is key because in such situations each person is presumably following his or her conscience. After all, trying to find the right way of acting is precisely what one who acts in conscience does. In the examples cited, we have someone following her conscience, but still getting it wrong. We might presume that she asked someone for advice about what to do, but that she still made her own decision in conscience and acted. Of course, she is obliged to follow her conscience. She makes the decision in conscience and still errs.

One could conjecture that she should have followed the other person's advice. Presumably she listened to it, but believed (correctly) that she still had to act the way her own conscience dictated. It told her, commanded her, to act as she did. She was and is bound to follow it.

DOES CONSCIENCE FREE US?

Too many people associate conscience with freedom, as in "I am free to follow my conscience." In one way that remark is correct; in other way, it is not. It is true to say "I am free to follow my conscience" in the sense that no one should force me to do otherwise. In the United States, for example, we are allowed to follow our consciences so long as we do not cause or do any harm. In the church, too, we are free to follow our consciences; the church does not want us to go against our consciences.

In another way, though, I am not free. I am not free *before* my conscience, to disobey or ignore it. Nor am I free to "not form" my conscience. Theological writing about conscience, in fact, rarely concerns freedom. Usually it speaks about the "dictates" of conscience or the "demands" of conscience. Conscience obliges or binds us.

Thomas Aquinas asked in the *Summa theologiae* whether anyone can ever go against one's own conscience. He answered, "never," adding that every time one does, one sins. His reasoning was simple: if we disobey our conscience what alternative is there for claiming that we are trying to find the right?

IS IT BAD TO BE WRONG?

Given that we are obliged to follow our consciences, what do we make of people (ourselves included) who follow their consciences with the intentions of doing good and acting out of love but get it wrong? Are they bad? If sin means badness (and it does) then we are in a lose-lose situation if we say that someone who doesn't follow her conscience sins and that someone who does, but gets it wrong, also sins. In our examples, then, the agent would be damned if she does and damned if she doesn't.

Thomas raised that question, too. He called it the question of the erroneous conscience: if someone follows her conscience and gets it wrong, is she bad? Thomas suggested that the reason why the person got the activity wrong is because she was ignorant. Thomas is right.

In all the examples we cited, the person did not know something. It wasn't because she didn't try or didn't care or didn't make an effort. It was because she didn't understand or recognize some-thing about a symptom, or behavior, or another's needs, or human nature.

When giving talks, I often ask parents whether there ever was a time they really tried to get something right but didn't. All the hands go up. They can look back at their lives and recognize mis-takes they made—not because they lacked love or effort or sincer-ity—but for lack of experience and the wisdom that comes with it. They had been "ignorant," just like the people in the cases we cited.

AQUINAS' ANSWER

Thomas answers the question, Is she bad when she was igno-rant? with another question: Why was she ignorant? He adds, if the person tried to understand but couldn't, then that is not sin. If, however, the person did not bother to learn what she should have known, she sins. Here Thomas gives us the key to the moral life: we must try to understand, to learn, to know what is the right and to do it. The key to morality is to strive to know the right and to do it. Otherwise, we are bad.

Before discussing what it means to strive to know the right, some readers may be asking what some call the Hitler (or Stalin) question: if you say that a person who follows her conscience is not bad, couldn't you argue that Hitler and Stalin were not bad if they claimed that they were following their consciences? It is really a ter-rible hypothesis.

I have pointed out that following conscience means trying to find out what is right. Can we actually believe it possible to claim to be looking for the right way of acting while at the same time killing, not just once, but for years, and killing not just a dozen people, but millions? Can we actually believe that Hitler acted "in conscience?" The enormity of his crimes against humanity, and the time they took, suggests that we ridicule conscience even to entertain the ques-tion. We can look at what those two figures did in this century and say with certainty that conscience was not operative. Their conduct was not from an erroneous conscience but from many years of failing to recognize that there is a conscience, one that needs to be formed and then obeyed. The Hitler question ought to be laid to rest.

We know that many times we seek to do the right and, despite adverse consequences, we are good. Yet whenever we fail to search for the right, regardless of the consequences, we are bad.

WHY THE SAMARITAN IS GOOD

The Gospels emphasize as much. For example, after Jesus gave the commandment to love God and neighbor as ourselves, he was asked, Who is my neighbor? In answer, he told the parable of the Good Samaritan. Only in passing does he mention those who robbed the man, for they are not the focus of his story. His main point concerns the people who do nothing. Their failure to respond to the neighbor is clearly sinful. They fail to bother, to find the right. The Samaritan, by contrast, finds it and does it.

Does the story change at all if the Samaritan stops to help but actually causes the victim more harm? Say, for example, that when the Samaritan put the injured man on his mule, the injured man slid off and cracked his skull? Is the "moral" of the parable different then? Or what if the Samaritan took him to the inn but the innkeeper was disreputable and hurt the man further? These questions are not meant to cause confusion, of course, but to entertain the question, Why is the Good Samaritan "good"?

The Samaritan is deemed good for trying to do the right. The others are bad because they failed even to look for it. It is as simple and as important as that.

The answer to the question I posed at the beginning of this essay—if you think an action is right but it isn't and you do it, are you bad?—then, is easy. It comes down to one word, "No!" But the converse can also be asked: "if you think its wrong (but it isn't) and you do it, are you good?" Of course, that answer is also "No!"

We can discuss as right or wrong the way we live and act. But goodness and badness are different. When it comes to who we are before God, what we do is not at the heart of the matter, but whether we love, whether we try, whether we strive, whether we bother. Morals, which are matters of love, are matters of effort.

CHAPTER FOURTEEN

Doing and Not Doing: The Key to Goodness

Growing up in Brooklyn was superb. My parish (everyone from Brooklyn refers to where they live by parish) was Saint Thomas Aquinas. We had a wonderful grammar school, despite sometimes having more than fifty or sixty students to a class. We were a very Catholic neighborhood. May crownings, Communion breakfasts, long processions, first Friday devotions, you name it, we were celebrating it. For children the best feast was All Saints. In our parish we not only had the opportunity to dress up on Halloween as our favorite Martian, ghoul, or witch, but on the next day, All Saints, we dressed up as the saint whose name we bore.

Every November 1, I looked like James the Greater. I had a beard since I was older (than the other James), a toga since that's what the apostles wore, and a walking staff since I traveled a great deal (was it to Spain?). My brother Bob dressed as a monk, with brown robes and a cord. I remember, too, that he was bald or so the iconography depicted him (though Bob wasn't too keen on the baldness). Our friend Peter looked pretty much like I did, except he dragged along the biggest set of keys you ever saw. And a kid named George had a huge plastic sword and kept looking for dragons. It was great fun.

SAINTS ACT

When I was growing up, we read the lives of the saints and learned what they did. This was key for our piety and devotion. Peter led the church; Thomas and James traveled and preached; Francis rebuilt the church; Elizabeth of Hungary took care of the poor; Catherine brought the Popes back to Rome; and Dominic preached. It was then that I learned what I now know to be true: that the key to understanding holiness is doing. Holy people do things. Yes, holy people hear God and listen and pray, but they also answer, act, and move. A sign of holiness is doing. God initiates certainly, but saints respond. Out of love for Christ, missionaries crossed seas, martyrs gave their lives, preachers faced their congregations, physicians healed, and teachers instructed. As Ignatius of Loyola once said, "Love shows itself in deeds rather than in words." The deeds of the saints, the great lovers of God, were nearly incredible.

Sometimes we have this rather naive view of the saints. We somehow sanitize them, make them normal, accessible, part of the crowd. But they aren't. Actually, most saints are rather peculiar, especially about what they do. Except for bitter herbs and the Eucharist, Catherine of Sienna basically gave up eating the last years of her life; her dying words were "Blood!" She was crying out for the blood of her Savior. Francis saw angels, talked to Christ crucified, stripped himself naked in his hometown, threw money at his bishop, and preached to birds. Peter Claver licked the sores of the slaves he tended in port cities. All of these saints tried to get as close to Christ as possible. That, in fact, is their holiness: seeking Christ through action. The great historian Caroline Bynum writes (in *Holy Feast and Holy Fast*), "Saints are not even primarily models for ordinary mortals; the saints are far too dangerous for that. Like Christ himself, they could not and should not be imitated in their full extravagance and power."

All saints seek to serve Christ. Whether Mother Teresa or Dorothy Day, the saint seeks to serve Christ in the world. Saints don't look for things to do; they don't have to. Instead they are alert, keep their eyes open, see enough of the tragedy of the world to respond to it. Often we find them ministering to the poor.

I met one such person, Sister Helen Prejean (I had read her book *Dead Man Walking: An Eyewitness Account of the Death Penalty in the United States*). She works with both those on death row and the families of their victims. She started this work in response to an invitation to write to one man on death row. She got involved in his life and death, and as he was executed, she sat before him as his spiritual director telling him, "Look on my face and see the face of Christ. Let the face of Christ be the face you see as you die." She has done this time and again and is passionate in her fight to rid our country of this practice. When I met her she was angry: though the Pope had narrowed the grounds somewhat in *Evangelium vitae*, he had still left the possibility of capital punishment open. Prejean is a woman who fights, moves, does. Such holy people stand in such stark contrast to those who don't.

RISKING A RESPONSE

Too often, in our contemporary Church, we fixate on a notion of holiness as simply avoiding wrong action. We think that goodness is simply not sinning. We have this easy notion of Christianity: if I avoid this or that, I'll avoid being bad. But as the Gospels let us know: there is nothing easy about Christianity. It is the religion of risk. It requires action, movement, response.

The medieval tradition had an important insight about this that guided much of their thoughts about goodness and badness. Gregory I wrote, "Certainly, in this world, the human spirit is like a boat foolishly fighting against the river's rush: one is never allowed to stay still, because unless one forges ahead, one will slide back downstream." Later Bernard of Clairvaux said, "on the way of life, to not progress is to regress." Finally Thomas Aquinas summarized the insight with his phrase: *In via Dei stare retrocedere est* ("To stand in the way of the Lord is to move backwards"). The call to follow Christ is the call to take steps. If one does not walk one does not follow. And when one does not follow, one sins.

This simple insight is often lost because we tend to think that evil or sin is something we actually do. But real sin is the failure to act, the failure to love. Admittedly, there are moments in the twentieth century when horrible things have been done: Hitler, Stalin, or Pol Pot come easily to mind. Like the deeds of serial killers, the brutality of such actions grips our imaginations in horror. But these are not the typical acts of sin. Typical sins are those in which we do not act. If we look at our own lives, we may see that our sin is often when we have not bothered to act.

FAUST: A NICE FAMILY MAN?

In a brilliant article entitled "Autobiography and Self-Deception," (*Truthfulness and Tragedy*, University of Notre Dame Press, 1977) David Burrell and Stanley Hauerwas look at the life of Albert Speer. Speer was a promising architect, recognized by Adolph Hitler, and commissioned to build in Nuremberg and Berlin. Speer was a "nice" man, a family man. He had none of the vicious, hate-driven obsessions that many leaders of the Third Reich (Goebbels, Goering, or Himmler, for example) possessed. He was basically a man interested in his architectural work, his career, and his family. He also was attracted to fame.

Speer was also particularly efficient. His efficiency assisted the Reich considerably when he was made minister of armaments in 1943. He took the collapsing Nazi forces and developed a way to get munitions to the front lines, protracting the war by nearly two years. It was not the treacherous thugs, the hateful leaders, who empowered the Nazis during the last years of their war; it was someone who really did not share their ideology, someone who had no ideology, someone who didn't hate. It was Speer, a man who was efficient, who did the work well because he enjoyed having Hitler's confidence and the architectural commissions he received. Speer traded his efficiency for fame, recognition, and contracts and became a modern-day Faust because he sold his soul to the devil, so to speak, for worldly glory.

Burrell and Hauerwas suggest that when we think of sinning we should think of Speer rather than Hitler because, chances are, we are probably more like Speer. Hitler sins, of course, but the sin of Speer is more ordinary, more familiar, more likely. It fits in with that haunting insight of Hannah Arendt about the "banality of evil." Give us the right place, the right time, the right conditions, and it may not take much for us to become a Speer, someone who sinned in what he didn't do. He didn't murder, torture, or rape; he didn't even hate or inflame passions. Speer's subordinates did not even approach him with the news of Nazi atrocities. Besides being efficient and seeking Hitler's approval, Speer's major activity was avoiding any knowledge of what the Nazis were doing. He did not want his life or his family's disturbed. In a word, he simply didn't bother himself with news of the monstrosities the Nazis were performing. And as minister of armaments this was not easy avoidance, for he was directly in charge of the "labor" camps.

Burrell and Hauerwas also suggest that Speer wanted life to be free of difficulties. The cross had no place on his horizon and so he did not bother to see it. Unlike saints who are known for their vigilance, Speer comfortably kept his head in the ground. Like us when we sin, Speer didn't want to be disturbed or bothered. His sin was ordinary, common, not mean-spirited. He was, however, the person most responsible for lengthening the war. He was the person most responsible for the death camps. How? He did nothing.

Ignatius suggests in *The Spiritual Exercises* that in meeting Christ in prayer we consider, What have I done for Christ? What am I doing for Christ? What will I do for Christ? I can't think of any better questions for understanding what goodness is about. For goodness, like "badness," is a question of whether we bother to respond to the Christ who calls us to follow him.

CHAPTER FIFTEEN

The Sin of Not Bothering to Love

While teaching at Fordham University, I lived in the dorms with undergraduates. I recall one great group of sophomores. Familiar with the lay of the land, they had gotten over their first-year homesickness and were pursuing their adult identities. They were a lot of fun, and I particularly enjoyed how they spoke about their parents. At the beginning of the year, they described their parents as "Joe and Jackie Cool," partly to win the interest of new classmates. But as their acquaintances and friendships developed, they would sometimes reveal that their parents had sometimes missed the mark. In a way, these students made their parents competitors, in that they were not going to make the same mistakes their parents had.

TWO TYPES OF PARENTAL MISTAKES

The students divided their parents' mistakes into two categories. First, there were the my-Mom-and-Dad-can-be-a-pair-of-klutzes stories—harmless, but humorous accounts centering on simple accidents or mistakes; such as Mom making a wrong turn or Dad forgetting something important. Of course, the stories were greatly embellished and sometimes complete fabrications, but through them these nineteen-year-olds could feel slightly superior to their absent (and undefended) parents. Their accounts also showed the listener that the narrator could be as much of a klutz as the parents were supposed to be (the fruit doesn't fall far from the family tree). These young people were struggling with adult challenges.

The other description of parental mistakes was neither humorous nor public. Rather, it involved confidential disclosures between roommates, friends, or lovers, sometimes painful accounts, probably a lot truer than the public, comic ones, about how shortcomings in one parent affected the life of this particular daughter or son. There were tales of a parent who drank too much, of one who worked hard but became frustrated and flew off the handle in anger, or a parent who was too timid to communicate adequately with spouse, employer, or child.

As the students began evaluating such mistakes, they dismissed the first set as simple error. Eventually, though, they wanted to know whether the harm caused by the second set meant that their parent did not love them. They wanted to figure out whether they meant anything to their overworked, under-confident, or obsessive parents. Assuredly the parent was wrong for drinking too much, blowing a fuse, or hiding out, but was that wrongness a sign that the parent did not love? Curiously, they did their best moral reasoning as they wrestled with this key question.

Eventually, they were able to admit the possibility that the parent may actually have been trying hard to be a good parent precisely when the personal problems erupted. Appreciating their parent as limited and recognizing their parent as capable of causing considerable harm, the students still saw that the parent may well have been trying to overcome timidity, wrestle with a demon, or tame an anger and, despite the struggle, still failed. They could even recognize in the parent's attempt to resist weakness, the power of his or her desire to be as loving as possible. The parent was wrong, but not because of any failure to love.

This insight was often matched by the student, long silent, with neither the comic nor sad stories of parental shortcomings. That student could remark that for him nothing had gone wrong, childhood had no crisis, and his parent was neither a klutz nor dysfunctional. As a matter of fact, he had been given a good deal, or so he thought. But now, listening to the struggles of his friends' parents he wasn't sure that his own parents had ever loved him, ever bothered with him. Could life have been so routinely facile that his parents never bothered to love?

The moment this fear was raised, the students knew that they were facing something terribly profound about human life. For not only were they faced with a peer who was uncertain about his parents' love, they were also glimpsing the insight that we can never simply presume from right or wrong activity that one is good or bad, loving or not.

WHO IS THE SINNER?

If we want to know what sin is, these students' insights are instructive. Who is the sinner in such stories? The parents who tried to be caring, responsible, and loving, but nevertheless caused harm, or the parents who did well but loved little? Clearly, I think sin is in the latter and not in the former. Sin is simply not bothering to love.

Not bothering to love is precisely the Gospel concept of sin. Jesus tells us that to love God and neighbor is the sum of the law. When someone asks him to clarify his teaching, Jesus tells the parable of the Good Samaritan. In it the one who loves is the Samaritan; those who fail to love—the priest and Levite—are sinners. Surprisingly we may notice that while Jesus has indicted (implicitly) the latter, he does not lead the listener to consider the wrongdoing of those who beat up the poor man on that famous road to Jericho.

In fact, throughout the Gospels, sin is not attributed to obvious wrongdoers, but consistently to those who don't bother to love. The parable of the rich man and Lazarus, for example, tells of a man who never bothered to notice his brother at the gate and who is punished for his negligence with hell fire. Similarly, the guest who fails to bother with the proper wedding garment is cast out to gnash his teeth. Matthew's last judgment separates the sheep from the goats, those who bothered to feed the hungry, clothe the naked, visit the imprisoned from those who did not bother and are condemned. Sin in the Gospels is always about not bothering to love.

Most people are able to recognize their own wrongdoing. We know, can easily name, and confess when we bad-mouth someone, indulge an obsession, let our anger fly, or act irresponsibly. But we don't so easily recognize our failures to love. In the Gospels the sinner is usually blind to the sinning. The rich man didn't realize his sinning. The "goats" ask where and when they had sinned. And even the famous Pharisee, standing in the Temple with the breast-beating Publican, is clueless to his own sinfulness.

NOT BOTHERING TO LOVE

Certainly one reason we are blind to our sinfulness is that for centuries we have held an overly simplistic view of sin: anything wrong that we did, we called sin. The very thing Christians are so familiar with we understand poorly. John Mahoney in his very important work, *The Making of Moral Theology* (Oxford, 1998), argues that we have "domesticated" sin. He is right. Were Jesus to return today, the parables he would tell about sinfulness would likely be the very same ones he told two thousand years ago, for like Jesus' contemporaries we, too, believe that sin is about wrongdoing and not about not bothering to love.

The other reason is that it is the nature of sin to blind us, to dull our senses. While causing harm may be easy to recognize (like the parental faults my students pointed out), it is difficult to spot a cold or uninterested heart. When our hearts are cold, dull, or lukewarm they can't tell us much. Like the goats, the rich man, the Levite, or the Pharisee, the hearts of sinners have not been "bothered" or "unsettled"; they are content, complacent, resting assured.

A German moral theologian Franz Boeckle argues in what appears to be reverse order that until we confess our sinfulness, we are blind to it. By confessing, we are illuminated; by actually naming where we did not bother to love we begin to see how deeply we sinned. The confession of sin is itself, Boeckle writes, "effective." It lets me the sinner know that I have sinned and how deeply. But if I don't confess, then I am like the Pharisee, thanking God that I am no Publican.

REGRET VS. REPENTANCE

In reflecting on the parents of my students, I am reminded of a wonderful distinction that another German moral theologian, Josef Fuchs, once made between regret and repentance. When people love and err they experience regret. Like the parents who make simple mistakes—the wrong turn, the wrong date, the wrong shirt size—they usually regret the error more than anyone affected by it. Likewise my students who told the painful stories were able to see how strongly their parents loved them precisely by the depth of their parents' regret for the harm they had caused. They saw in their parents' faces or heard in their words of apology, the depth of love that prompted their regret. Loving people regret the harm their shortcomings cause.

Repentance, though, is different. Unlike regret, which comes from within the loving person, repentance usually comes as a summons from without. It challenges us to see where we did not bother to strive, to grow, to love. Unlike regret that usually comes precisely from those areas where we are weak, repentance addresses those areas of our lives where we are strong—namely, where we could have bothered, where we were able. In those areas of our lives the call to repentance asks, could we have tried more or better?

Too easily we associate sin with weakness, but in the Gospel sin occurs precisely where one is strong. The rich man could have shared his riches, the priest and the Levite could have taken care of the wounded man, the "goats" could have responded to the neighbor in need. Most of us try our hardest precisely where we are weakest, but the story of sin, like the call to repentance, concerns those areas of our lives where we could have tried harder, precisely because we were so able. Christ judges not the weak heart that struggles, but rather the strong one that does not bother. As my students realized, we sin out of strength, not weakness.

CHAPTER SIXTEEN

Are You As Good As You Think You Are?

While enjoying a wonderful sabbatical at the Center of Theological Inquiry in Princeton, I celebrated my forty-second birthday. A friend drove up from Washington and together we shared a great dinner and a nice bottle of wine while we caught up on how our lives have been going.

I couldn't help but notice how happy I am compared to twenty years ago. The difference, I think, is remarkable. Today I'm a lot more focused about my work, my friends, my vocation. I choose what I do more freely and more deliberately. I can work on a variety of projects with greater ease and enjoyment. I'm more reliable with my family and friends and appreciate whatever time I can have with them. I sleep better. I'm more confident and a lot less compulsive. The goals I set today, I often attain. When I think of myself twenty years ago, I had a lot of goals and incredible drives and was bothered by many different personal concerns.

You are probably recognizing the same changes in yourselves. After all, with years of experience, work, and relationships, reflection and maturity ought to enable us to understand and live life better. We may be more tired than we once were, but we are also a lot more able today to do most things that we couldn't consistently do then.

We are, I think, more virtuous today than we were twenty years ago. If prudence means taking the right steps into the future to guarantee growth, the choices we make today are more prudent—steadier, more appropriate, and more successful than our decisions years ago. We are likewise more just. During the war in Vietnam, perhaps, we may have had a more passionate inter- est in the issues of war and peace, but today we are more aware of the diverse responsibilities we have. Similarly, we are familiar with our natural propensity to avoid those responsibilities.

Today, we take steps to keep our feet in place whenever we have the urge to flee. After twenty years of living with family and friends, we are better at maintaining relationships and nurturing them. We've learned from caring spouses, pastors, and friends what real faithfulness is. We also know more about self-care. Certainly, we may still have a number of liabilities—being overweight, touched with neurosis, and some high blood pressure, maybe—but we are also probably more patient with ourselves and less inclined to the more brutal self-assessments that we made two decades ago.

Despite our aging bodies, as persons we are probably all a lot bet- ter off today than we were twenty years ago. In that way, I'm sure that we are also more virtuous. But does that assessment mean that we are more morally good? If we say that we are more prudential, just, faith- ful, and self-caring, are we also claiming to be morally better?

BEING RIGHT ISN'T THE SAME AS BEING GOOD

Certainly, in one way we are morally better. We are more rightly ordered. We are more able to anticipate and address a variety of personal and social issues. We are, on balance, more integrated, per- sonally and morally. But that rightness aside, are we more good? Are we holier? More meritorious? More worthy because we are so much more virtuous? I really don't know.

When I think of the fervor and dedication I had years ago, I marvel at all the good will I had, dysfunction aside. When I think of the openness I had, the willingness to tolerate discomfort for the sake of a just cause, the resilience in the face of adversity, and the generosity albeit with plenty of mixed motivations, I am not at all sure that I am more morally good or more loving today with all my virtues, than I was back then with my many vices.

In moral theology, we make a distinction between what I do and what I could do, between attaining and striving, between being right and being good. We are more able to do the right, to be virtuous, to be rightly ordered today than twenty years ago. But are we actually more loving? Are we striving more than twenty years ago?

In the past, because we were more prone to getting things wrong, to acting or speaking irresponsibly, to making a fool of ourselves and others, we hesitated to think of ourselves as morally good. Not feeling confident about ourselves, we could resonate with the Gospel parable of the prodigal son. We knew that we could apologize again and again and, as Jesus told Peter, we would be forgiven and made good again. We never dared to think of ourselves as the Pharisee in the Temple because we felt at ease being the Publican. Though we were more likely twenty years ago to be intemperate, cowardly, rude, overbearing, or even manipulative, still we were modest about our own moral assessment. Trapped as many young people are by competing self-interests, we were not presumptuous about grace or goodness.

But today because we are more responsible, we are not as prone to damaging our lives or others. We do not find ourselves returning home with so many feelings of shame and confusion—we have not been out spending Dad's estate on lecherous living. Rather we have become the prodigal's older brother, returning home from work tired from a focused life, from a hard-won and effectively ordered life. We have learned to stay in our Father's house, enjoying many blessings. And we have learned a great many skills.

A NEW, POTENTIALLY DANGEROUS MATURITY

Now, as virtuous, we do things better than we ever did. We have learned how to act maturely, to administer, to mediate difficulties, to remain in control. But in the process, we can fall prey to self-deception, thinking that because we are more rightly ordered, more virtuous, we are more morally good.

The Gospels remind us that to those who have been given more, more will be expected. Over these twenty years we have had opportunities for growth that many do not. It may be true that we have taken advantage of them and developed ourselves, but now because we are capable of more, more is expected.

I am not making a Pelagian claim here. We ought not be driven to exhaustion, to earning our salvation, to blasphemous attempts at saving ourselves. But by the same token we ought to be modest about our self-understanding. In terms of rightness, we might be more upright. In terms of goodness, we might not necessarily be more loving. We need to see, therefore, that we are subject to the vice of self-deception: we can deceive ourselves into thinking that our rightly ordered lives are signs of moral superiority.

A Look at These Dangers from a Variety of Perspectives

Many of us grew up in a religious culture that did little to help us with self-esteem. We learned pathetic lessons of false humility, self-loathing, and a variety of other neurotic tendencies. These lessons were as ironic as they were harmful. For we come from a religious tradition claiming that we are made in the divine image, that our creation was judged very good, indeed, by God, that God so loved us that Christ died for us, that God redeemed us, and that God wants to spend eternity with us. Yet somehow our culture was not communicating this. Instead of deriving our self-understanding from the light of faith, we looked at our humanity not as a gift but as a burden.

Today, we suffer from a milieu that is positively addicted to self-affirmation. Wanting to undo the centuries of neurotic conditioning of the faithful, proponents of a new spirituality praise the human. But this movement remains free of divine insight. For just as we once judged poorly our humanity without any recollection of scriptural claims, so today we esteem our humanity without them. When we judge ourselves morally, the Gospels tell us, we must do it from God's perspective.

Nonetheless, some are adding divine insight to their successes, equating their personal success with God's will. Though some Christian believers have at times associated personal prosperity with God's favor, Catholics have always resisted the presupposition. Catholics have long believed in the Gospel phrase that "the rain falls on the just and the unjust." We know too well that neither success nor misfortune indicates that one is responding to grace. We also know that, as in the case of Job, terrible things can happen to good people. Just as disorder is no sign of being bad, the right order in one's life is no sign of being good.

What we can say about our lives now is that we have been blessed. For our lives are not personal achievements. They are testimonies to the many who have given us courage, wisdom, support, resources, love, and opportunities to serve the church well. What we have now in our lives is not an accomplishment, but a gift. It is an insight that we often miss.

CHAPTER SEVENTEEN

On Knowing Goodness and Rightness

Rightly or wrongly, Catholics have always been modest about knowing about salvation: we believe that no one can know with certitude that they are good or saved.

I've always found that teaching terribly important because it resonates with my own experience. I believe that I am saved by Jesus Christ and I hope in God's mercy that when I die I will be raised up on the Last Day. I believe similarly that the offer of salvation is made to everyone. But I also believe that I really do not know how well I am responding to all God's grace that comes into my life. Am I really receiving God's grace, am I responding in faith to Christ, am I striving as best I can? I really do not know. In fact, as I made clear in the previous essay, I don't think I will know the answer about my goodness in this life. That, after all, is what the first letter of John suggests when he says that "we shall be like God for we shall see ourselves as we are." Even if I turn out worse than I had hoped, still I trust and hope in God's mercy.

The modesty is not at all pretentious. As a matter of fact, we should call it simple ignorance. Whether we are good or bad, whether we strive as best we can for the right or not, is really beyond our knowing. We know of this inability, not only from our own experience, but from the Gospels as well. On Judgment Day, Matthew 25 tells us the sheep will be separated from the goats. And the Lord will say to those on his right: "Enter my kingdom, because you fed me, clothed me, sheltered me." "But when?" the sheep ask. They have no idea of how the grace of God has flourished in their lives. Like a mustard seed, like yeast, their goodness has grown greatly and secretly.

Likewise, those on the left side do not know about why they were condemned. "When did we not feed you or clothe you?" They just didn't know. Nor did the rich man and Lazarus. He is damned to hell fire: "Tell my brothers!" he cries out.

This can jar us. We believe, or so some would have us believe, that we cannot sin unless we know it. Aha! Guess what? Everyone condemned in Matthew 25 didn't know that they sinned and not only were they convicted of sin but they were eternally damned! Like Dives, like the five foolish virgins, like the man who hoarded the one talent, they didn't know that they were about to loose, big time! And we, like them, have put such a commodity on knowledge and autonomy, that we actually believe that, if we don't know about it, we can't be called sinners. We could get away with murder, so long as we didn't know about it. That was, after all what Speer tried to do.

I remember being disturbed about this years ago. I was only ten years old and was walking home from Church in Brooklyn with my grandma Goodwin. "Grandma, I learned that you can't commit a mortal sin unless it's grave matter, full knowledge and full consent of the will." (Yes, at those times even ten-year-olds understood those words, it was Catholic talk!) "That's right, Jimmy." "Well, if that's the case, then it's pretty hard to commit a mortal sin. I mean who has full consent and full knowledge of anything" "That's right, Jimmy. It's nearly impossible to commit a mortal sin."

I was baffled. We made our moral accountability contingent on whether we knew what was going on. But that's not the way it works. Jesus challenged that and, more recently, Nuremberg challenged that. There's a lot that we don't know and we should.

TWO THINGS FOR CHRISTIANS TO THINK ABOUT WITH REGARD TO KNOWLEDGE

Christians should think about what they cannot know and what they should know. What we can't know is how good or bad we are; what we need to find out is what is the right thing to do. Any attempt at the first is no more than what I call moral narcissism; the second, however, is precisely our moral task. Let me explain.

In the previous essays we saw that being good is actually striving for the right as best we can. Thus to respond to Christ's call is to find out how we can become more rightly ordered or virtuous so that we can together with others make the world a better place. We are charged with the responsibility to learn how to bring about more rightness in our lives. So, yes, we are required to know how we can become better able to respond to our brothers and sisters in need, how we can bring about greater virtue in the world, how we can promote justice. That's what we mean by pursuing the command of God. We need to know how to pursue the right.

What we cannot know is how hard we are really striving to find the right. As I wrote earlier, that self-knowledge escapes us. We cannot know the integrity of our moral effort. We may think we do, we may even try to do it; but as John's epistle suggests: we cannot know it now, in this life. If we think we know it, we are only (dangerously) kidding ourselves. I say dangerously because we could on the one hand give ourselves false comfort, on the other hand we could be too hard on ourselves.

Like Jesus, we are called always to move forward. Certainly we can on occasion reflect on when we tried to do something and got it wrong. We can discover our errors and, then we can express regret, as Fuchs would say, and subsequently find a way of getting it right. *But,* finding out whether our conduct is right or wrong, is different from finding out whether we are good or bad.

Christ forgives us as sinners, that is, Christ forgives us our badness precisely so that we are free to move forward. We may not know how bad we really are, but we can be sure that to some degree we are bad. But we can live with the reasonable assertion that even though I can't know how good or bad I am, I can at least be sure that I am somewhat bad. We can live with that assertion because Christ in his mercy forgives us that badness, that failure to love. How often? Seven Times? Yes, seventy times seven times.

Christ forgives us our sins to leave us free to *keep* following him. Christ continues to beckon us to pursue the right, by forgiving whenever we do not. But Christ also warns us against thinking our-selves good. Like the one Pharisee who thanks God that he is not like the Publican, we need to be mindful that we do not falsely deceive ourselves about our moral goodness. Certainly we should be thankful that Christ "has saved such a wretch as me," but that I am saved by Christ's mercy is a lot more different than that I am good.

I am often struck by the fact that saints, as they get older, realize that there is plenty for them to be thankful for because of God's mercy; as they grow in this wisdom, they also grow in the self-understanding that they are probably not as good as they thought they were. These people who never suffered from any loss of self-esteem simply realize that, like the rest of us, they are sinners. They liked themselves, but notwithstanding that, they also knew that they were sinners. I remember living for a summer with Horace McKenna in Washington, D.C. He would think that any talk of him as good was rubbish. Likewise, Dorothy Day, as she got older, often said that she was surprised at really how petty she was. As people get closer to God, they realize that most of the light is radiating from God onto themselves, and not, vice versa.

A THIRD THING FOR CHRISTIANS TO KNOW

As Christians learn that they can't know how good or bad they are and that any attempt to know this is vainglorious, they also learn that they ought to spend their time more profitably finding out what the right course of living is. Simultaneously a third insight emerges. Whereas we can know (to some extent) whether a person's conduct is right or wrong, we cannot know how bad or good they are either. This was the other fault of the story of the pious Pharisee: not only did he think himself good, he also thought the Publican was bad.

The distinction between goodness and rightness sets us on the correct track. It tells us that we can know a great deal about wrong-ness and rightness, in fact a lot more than we have bothered to know. But it also tells us that our temptation to know the degree of goodness or badness about ourselves or another is an idle temptation. It calls us to invest ourselves into making ourselves and the world more right.

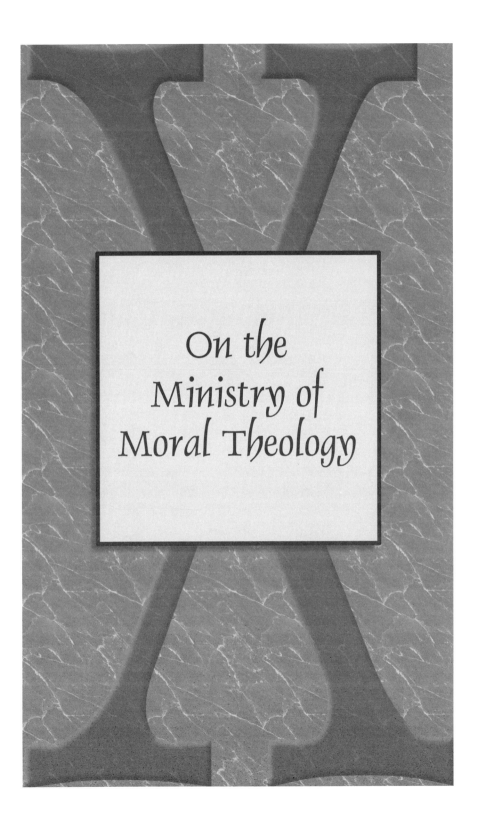

On the
Ministry of
Moral Theology

CHAPTER EIGHTEEN

On Giving Moral Advice

To students preparing for priesthood and lay ministry, I teach the dreaded subject of moral theology at Weston Jesuit School of Theology. They are intelligent, articulate, and in love with their respective vocations. But they are demanding: they insist that what I teach is relevant to their future pastoral work. They have made me a better teacher and theologian by directing me toward always integrating theory and practice.

One of the basic works that they and, in fact, all of us face regards moral advice. In making moral decisions, all of us either consult or are consulted. Since that moral task—above all others—integrates theory and practice, let me share with you some of the fundamental insights that I have learned about such advising.

1. *Listen.* I frequently get calls from people of conscience wanting to find out whether their way of deliberating about a particular matter is right. The caller begins explaining something about bookkeeping, genetic structures, surgical devices, legal appeals, or union balloting. After one minute, I stand in fright and wonder, "what on earth is this person going to ask?" At that moment I realize again how little competence I have.

It's common to critique priests as knowing nothing about sex and marriage. Some remark, "Why talk to priests about sex and marriage when they know nothing about it?" I marvel that the charge stops there! I'm incompetent on most professional matters but people still ask my advice about all sorts of matters, including sex and marriage. This may be because I've learned to listen and to recognize how competent my callers are not only about balances, molecular biology, and torts, but also about moral reasoning. And they, like so many people, want someone whose reasoning and listening they trust as well.

In 1983, after my first year of graduate studies in moral theology, my dad's former partner from the New York Police Department called me. His two nieces had been in a car accident a year earlier. One walked away fine; the other was critically injured. For a year she had been on a rotating bed that helped her breathe and attached to a respirator. Since the accident, this twenty-year-old woman had never regained consciousness and had been resuscitated more than six times. The parents tried for a year to win her recovery, sparing no expense or devotion. But after the mother had spent a full year sleeping in the hospital by her daughter's bedside, they began to understand that she would never come back to them. Not knowing how to let go of their daughter, they asked for my advice. I discovered that while all my knowledge about extraordinary means, benefits, and burdens was fresh, their way of proceeding did not easily conform to my ways of training. At first, they rejected a Do Not Resuscitate (DNR) order, terrified that in the event that their daughter had another seizure, she would come out of her coma and hear the doctors say, "Her parents refuse to have her resuscitated." Later, they gave up their fear and ordered the DNR. She suffered another seizure, but an intern on duty resuscitated her without reading the chart. In spite of this, they were unable to consider another option, removing her from the respirator. They understood that the respirator was "extraordinary," but they considered the action too direct because of the likelihood of her death soon after its removal. Finally, they decided to stop the bed's rotation. She died quietly several days later. They needed to figure out in their own way, with their own reasoning, how to let go of their daughter. I learned from them.

How we reason is a very human process. If we are to advise then, we must learn to listen. We must learn to discover the ways others reason. And we learn this from the people we serve. As we learn to listen, we will grow in competence. Along the way, it may be good also to remember that unlike Catherine of Siena, who learned Latin overnight by divine inspiration, most of us will spend our lives acquiring competency to listen and learn.

2. *Be positive.* The best of moral theology appeared when teachers and preachers talked primarily about goals and virtues, and not about sin or wrong ways of acting. In the patristic period, in the writings of Saints Francis of Assisi, Albert the Great, and Thomas Aquinas, and in the modern era with the writings of the Second Vatican Council, we see the call to heed the Scriptures and to follow Jesus' call to discipleship. We must encourage people to look forward in their pursuit of the Lord. And if, like Lot's wife, they insist on looking back and begin worrying about wrongness and sin and what they should avoid, we may remind them that sinners in the New Testament are always known not for what they do, but for what they *fail* to do, for failing to bother. The love command in the Scriptures is rarely about avoiding action; it's about acting.

3. *Invite people to set goals.* Often we live in the world of ER, where every instance of moral thought and action looks like a reaction. Sure, moral dilemmas often look like an unanticipated problem arriving on a gurney, but much of life concerns the expected. Consider, for example, that parents decide on schools for their children or that students themselves choose courses. A good deal of our life is spent designing, dreaming, and planning. The moral life is not usually about a catastrophe that has just occurred.

One way to help people to be pro-active in moral living is to ask them what we call the three "virtue questions": "Who are you?" "Who do you want to become?" "How can you get there?" By inviting people to understand themselves better and to set goals, we can help them to reason better as moral individuals. Remember, in most areas of life—family, financial, leisure, and work—people make plans about what *they* will do; we can invite them to think similarly about the moral life.

4. *Talk about the virtues.* One way of setting goals is to ask people whether they want to become more just, faithful, self-caring, or prudent. Parents, in particular, love the virtues, because in parenting they look for ways to teach their children about fairness and friends and family. Thus they help them form friendships, play with siblings, take care of themselves and respect property. Through a variety of exercises, from hosting birthday parties and planning family outings to setting times for study, television, and bedtime, parents establish habitual patterns of action that guide their children through their lives. Those exercises are the stuff of virtue.

5. *Respect the conscience.* Thomas Aquinas, at an early stage of his teaching ministry, argued that Peter Lombard was wrong to claim that if Church and conscience conflict, one should obey always the former. The young Aquinas wrote boldly in his *Commentary on the Fourth Book of the Sentences of Peter Lombard*, "here the Master (Lombard) is wrong, it is better to die excommunicated than to violate the conscience." Our tradition has always included a strong, continuous argument upholding the primacy of the conscience. Certainly some have misused this teaching, giving people license to do whatever they wish. But the primacy of the conscience means that each person is responsible to form and follow it. Be mindful, though, of those who qualify this primacy. They, like Peter Lombard, fail to see that each disciple must answer the call of Christ at the depth of her or his very own being. Any compromise of the primacy of conscience compromises then the very possibility of that call.

6. *Don't solve people's problems; rather, help them form their own consciences.* We should see every occasion that someone asks us for advice as an opportunity for helping the questioner look at larger questions, which can help them to be more self-reliant and self-directed. This is important. Moral progress always occurs when people take steps of their own and in their own way. Consider when Rosa Parks took her place on the bus in Montgomery, when Thomas More refused to take the Oath of Supremacy, when Martin

Luther King, Jr., wrote to white preachers on scraps of paper in a Birmingham jail, when Gdansk shipyard workers decided to strike for their rights, or when the faceless Chinese student stepped forward to meet an oncoming tank in Tianamen Square. In each instance, a person moved history and humanity forward with a conscience that demanded personal action. But, remember that every conscience will be different. As we listen and help people to set their goals, we also must respect the integrity of the conscience as the place where each person hears the voice of God.

Mark Twain understood this when he described Huck Finn's conflict prompted by (what Huck called) his "conscience." Formed by the community that he came from, Huck's "conscience" required him under pain of damnation to respect God and neighbor and to let poor "Ole Miss Watson" know the whereabouts of her slave Jim. Reluctantly, he composed a letter, but soon after he thinks of Jim not as Miss Watson's "property," but as his companion. He remembers what Jim has done for him and what he has done for Jim, and how much the two of them have learned together about life and friendship. He continues . . .

> and at last I struck the time I saved him by telling the men we had small-pox aboard, and he was so grateful, and said I was the best friend old Jim ever had in the world, and the only one he's got now; and then I happened to look around, and see that paper.
>
> It was a close place. I took it up, and held it in my hand. I was trembling, because I'd got to decide, forever, betwixt two things, and I knowed it. I studied a minute, sort of holding my breath, and then says to myself:
>
> "All right, then, I'll go to hell"—and tore it up.

Huck's own experience challenges the "conscience" of the community and prompts him to act as his own man.

7. *Remember the parable of the Good Samaritan.* Concretely, this parable accentuates the difficulty we feel while rushing to our jobs and passing homeless people asking for handouts. On one level the parable never lets us feel comfortable. It reminds us that we have many neighbors in need. The parable never lets us fall into self-complacency, but rather calls us to greater vigilance and attentiveness. For this reason, the great ethicist Stanley Hauerwas reminds us that Christians must always be watchful, on constant alert.

On another level we see the very surprising answer to the original question posed to Jesus "Who is my neighbor?" What is the answer? Isn't it, "the one who showed mercy?" Too often, when we think of the parable, we believe that the neighbor is someone who needs to be helped; but in the Gospel Jesus teaches us that our neighbor is the one who shows mercy. In my own life, I know the importance of having neighbors like the Good Samaritan. One friend of mine is a pastor in a poor neighborhood in Boston who routinely faces the terrible burdens of working with people constantly marginalized by political and economic machinations. Another is a Jesuit physician who has worked for ten years in the AIDS unit of Boston City Hospital and is preparing for work in Uganda. As I work and teach in Cambridge I need friends and neighbors like that. We all do.

8. *Be attentive to distinctions.* It is the great Jesuit legacy to recognize and heed the claims of distinctions. And we are correct to stress them, because often when we hear that moral issues are complicated, we seek too easily simple solutions. Pat answers are usually inaccurate. Simply gliding over circumstances with some general principle is not helpful. Remember, too, Aquinas' important insight: general principles apply generally. Nothing more, nothing less. No one is worse on this topic than the media, who love reminding their listeners that any serious issue they present is "very complicated" but who insist that the solutions be describable in a micro-second.

Usually taking a person off a life support system is not killing a person, but letting them die; telling a person who is HIV positive and refuses to abstain from sexual relations that he should use a condom is not promoting sexual activity, but protecting the common good; and tolerating a morally wrong activity is not the same as doing the wrong activity. If morality is about understanding who we are and what we ought to do, then for starters we ought to be careful about describing what we do. Sloppy descriptions do not help in moral advising.

9. *Be responsible with Church teaching.* Rome is complicated; her history is complex. There is nothing disrespectful in seeking accuracy, whether about the way the Church exercises her authority at a given moment or about the historical claims she makes for a particular teaching. As ministers, we are passing on a tradition that is not the dead faith of the living, but the living faith of the dead. That living historical tradition must be handed on with integrity. Moreover, history concerns the progress of humanity and in that progress there is growth. Thus, on moral matters our perspective develops and even changes. For example, a wise rector in Rome remarked to me that if *in vitro* fertilization were available in the seventeenth century, that is, if they had then the technology by which a woman could conceive a child without sex, the Church would have not simply permitted the technology, but would have *mandated* it! In the seventeenth century most moralists and bishops were so convinced of the probable moral harm that resulted from sexual union that they easily would have endorsed separating the procreative act from the unitive act, a position that Rome holds untenable today.

Finally, we must always remember that moral teaching, at any level of the Church, comes from human beings. We should listen to the Church, but as educated adults, not as timid children or as reactionary teenagers.

10. *Avoid the slippery slope argument.* We learned this argument when we were children. We would ask our parents if just this one

night we could stay up later and they would say, "No, because tomorrow you'll ask to stay up even later." We knew then (and we forget it often enough today) that the "slippery slope" is the worst moral argument. The slippery slope is always used by people in power. Upon hearing a request or a proposal, they dismiss it as dangerous: it will likely undermine authority, cause chaos, and unleash moral turpitude. The argument is, then, designed simply to preclude, foreclose, and dismiss. We use it often; we shouldn't. It is nothing more than heavy-handedness. Any authority that we enjoy will depend on whether others find in us an openness necessary for reflection.

11. *Use reason.* Whether we agree or disagree with peers, employees, superiors, or pastors, let the rightness of our positions be guided by good, concrete, rational thinking. It is after all what the Roman theologian Josef Fuchs, and before him, Thomas Aquinas called the natural law. A good argument is based on right reason. Let that be our final arbiter.

Some people might ask, "Is that all there is?" But, that's all there has ever been. In his Letter to the Romans Saint Paul wrote that all people, even those who have not yet heard the Word of God preached, know to distinguish right from wrong. In our capacity to reason well, God has given us the facility and the task to discover what betters our lives and what harms it. God placed us out of the Garden, but blessed us with the ability to reflect, understand, judge, and decide. That ability to reason well is precisely our moral guide.

12. *Share doubts.* When we fear that a particular proposal will lead to all sorts of difficulties, we can share those fears. Here we can use slippery slope language, not as an argument or as the last word, but as expressing our initial concerns. We can say things like, "I'm concerned that what you're suggesting will have terrible consequences." But let that fear and doubt be the beginning of the conversation, not its end. By being honest with our initial assessments, we give others the opportunity to know what we are really thinking and to respond in kind.

We should also not be afraid to express our own doubts about our own abilities. We are not perfect. I remember when I first started teaching at Weston, if a student disagreed with me, I used all my skills to "respond," hoping that the student would not dare to disagree again. I was inexperienced, intimidated, and defensive. Now with more confidence and experience, I welcome their judgments as well as their questions. Their questions open up new areas of reflection, other times they prompt me to reconsider my own positions, and sometimes they leave me in the dark, and that's when I answer, "I don't know." I am no longer afraid of uttering those words. None of us should be.

13. *We become what we do.* Today we tend to think of morality as only about big actions: abortion, euthanasia, grand theft, etc. But for Aquinas, almost everything we do is a moral action. He wrote, "a human act is a moral act." He realized that morality is about human living and that morality views all actions as opportunities that shape us for better or worse. By our actions, we work out the people we eventually become. If we are condescending with people, we will become more arrogant. If we are habitually sloppy in our thinking, we will become even sloppier. If we struggle to listen, we will eventually listen better. If we take time to pray, we will be more open to God's ways.

We must get into the habit of thinking of our ministry as an opportunity not only to serve others, but also as a chance to become the people we want to be. By learning to advise well, we assist our colleagues, friends, students, or employees to judge better, but we also form ourselves into competent and thoughtful people. Toward that end, we must listen to our hearts and anticipate every encounter as a fresh moment that allows us to become more that disciple whom Jesus calls.

CHAPTER NINETEEN

Listening to the Voice of Suffering

In the face of another's suffering, how should we act? In order to answer this question, we need to know how both the Hebrew Bible and the Gospels consider suffering. As in every religion, there is a deep desire to overcome suffering, for no religion considers suffering as good in itself. In the Hebrew Bible, for instance, the Israelites distinguished between the suffering we bring on ourselves and "unmerited suffering." According to them, we sometimes suffer from our own fault and sometimes from no fault of our own. That no-fault, unmerited suffering, was the particular object of the Israelites' concern, for at times they suffered without cause. In the face of such unmerited suffering, they were perplexed precisely because they believed in a Provider God. How could the faithful suffer if God provides? Precisely because of their belief, they did not hesitate to direct hard questions to God. "Is God asleep?" asks Psalm 44.

Christians, too, see God as opposed to suffering, precisely in the person of Jesus. Through his miracles, Jesus regularly frees people from their suffering. And, by his death and resurrection he conquers death and frees us from its clutches. Like other religions, the Christian response to suffering is to find a way of eliminating it.

MERITED SUFFERING

But the Gospels steer us away from any distinction between merited and unmerited suffering. Certainly many times we think we can assume the reason for another's suffering: too much smoking, being overweight, hanging out with the wrong crowd, and so on. When we assume that we can identify the cause of another's suffering, however, Jesus confronts us with the stories of the man born blind (Jn 9:2f.) and of the murdered Galileans (Lk 13:1–5). Are we sure we know why the man was born blind? Are we sure why the Galileans were murdered?

Certainly we may know a friend or relative who had no sense of self-preservation or regard for others. Certainly, in those instances of clarity, where one's suffering could be alleviated, we have the responsibility to confront the person with her recklessness. But the narratives of human suffering are rarely written in the clear and evident ink of recklessness. And those few privileged instances of knowing the cause of an intimate's suffering, do not give us insight into the cause of everyone else's suffering. Jesus challenges us with the question: are we competent to discern whose suffering is merited and whose is not?

This insight from the Gospels has practical significance. Certainly, God can distinguish merited from unmerited suffering, but we rarely can. This is because the line between merited and unmerited suffering is hardly ever clear. How can we know that someone's suffering is really "unmerited"? Does the AIDS victim have to be a child or a hemophiliac? Does the cancer victim really have to have taken every precaution against carcinogens? Must the tortured activist have been politically prudent? Does the date rape victim really have to insist "No" the entire evening? Is it only in the face of absolute innocence that we declare a sufferer as suffering without merit?

WHY WE BLAME THE SUFFERER

I suggest that with a little self-examination we might discover other reasons for why we are quick to blame others for their own suffering. I add that as pastoral ministers we are products of the culture in which we live. We engage in the same practices.

First, as Americans we tend to believe that suffering can always be abolished. We see it in health prevention issues: we believe that all cardiac conditions are eliminated by diet or exercise, that all genetic difficulties can be screened away, that all addictions are treatable by twelve-step programs, that all injuries are subject to perfect healing. Likewise we eliminate other problems that cause suffering: abortion removes the unwanted pregnancy, jails remove lawbreakers and on occasion we use capital punishment to eliminate their presence all together, and now we move to euthanasia to eliminate any process to dying. No one, we think, should have to suffer; it's their own fault if they do.

Second, following from this belief that suffering can be eliminated, we contend that suffering is rarely unmerited in the first place. How many of us have attended wakes and heard (or remarked) he shouldn't have smoked; shouldn't have kept that job; should have rested more; was always too tense, grossly overweight, never exercised, and so on. As ministers, we should be stunned at the ease with which our congregations (and sometimes we ourselves) carelessly attribute the deceased's demise to the deceased's own hand. It is as if no one dies anymore of a variety of causes. (Behind this is the belief that if only we did not lack will power and decision making, we would live forever.)

Third, as a society we are convinced of the singular importance of self-reliance. Everyone can succeed. If you do not, it is your own fault. Thus we have generated an enormous system of hateful rhetoric in order to accommodate the "American myth." Any failure by an African-American is attributed to laziness, by a woman to weakness, by a gay man to neurosis, and so on. This stance escalates even more so when we talk about people beyond our borders, especially the third world.

Finally, we don't tolerate complex explanations. When something goes wrong, we want to know the bottom line: why did it happen? who's at fault? Long stories are simple obfuscations.

We are as a people fixed on the belief that suffering is merited. As ministers we could invite our congregations to ask themselves why it is we so deeply hold on to that presupposition and why we have such a difficult time not understanding Jesus' question.

Let me be clear here. I am not arguing that no one is in any measure accountable for her or his suffering, nor that we should not attempt to correct or alleviate suffering. What I am insisting on is that before the sufferer even speaks, we believe we know the cause of people's suffering: themselves. That is the belief that Jesus challenges in the Gospel. Moreover, as a belief, it often makes us terrible listeners to another's suffering, and, that fact often compounds the narrator's suffering.

COMPASSIONATE LISTENING

The act of listening compassionately encourages the sufferer to speak. Encouraging the sufferer to speak is a very biblical stance. Nowhere is this clearer than in the book of Job. There we see the calamities of Job—children killed, property destroyed, body infected. Because the suffering is so great, Job's friends are convinced that it must be merited. His "friends" surround him, inhibit him from claiming innocence, and try to redirect the purpose of his discourse. The only one who gives Job a "hearing" is God. God allows Job to speak.

The same listening stance is found in the Gospels as Jesus hangs on the cross. Along with Mary, John, and Mary Magdalen, God hears the cry of Jesus, "My God, my God, why have you forsaken me?" We may think with Jesus that God is not listening, that God has abandoned Jesus. But Jesus senses death the same way all human beings do, with a radical sense of entering it alone. But God never abandons him: indeed, God raises him up on the third day.

God listens to the cry of the sufferer. Of course, in the face of God's silence we might ask God, "Are you asleep?" But God's silence both in Job and at the crucifixion conveys, instead, a God both attentive and listening.

THE IMPORTANCE OF EXPRESSING ONE'S SUFFERING

The call for us to listen to one who is suffering is not an easy one, for it presupposes that the sufferer can or will speak. We can learn to apprise such suffering through the sufferer's own movements. But we can develop this sense only when the listener has been attentive to the nature of suffering in her/his own life. That is, if we are aware of the narrative of suffering within our own bodies, we can learn to listen to another's own narrative of suffering. Revisiting the terrain of one's own suffering establishes the groundwork for becoming a compassionate and perceptive listener.

That the body expresses suffering is very important. Nonetheless, the body, in all its pain prefers to express itself through the voice. Even when the sufferer cannot voice in any *articulate* way her/his suffering, still the voice wants to *utter* its suffering. We can turn to the psalms of lament which do not attempt to explain or give meaning to suffering, but rather give voice to the anguish, rage, and despair that the sufferer experiences. The sufferer, unable to express or name the particularity of her suffering, is still able to acknowledge to some extent its depth. Likewise, reciting these psalms for one unable to speak provides the sufferer with a surrogate voice.

GIVING VOICE TO PAIN

Nowhere has this relationship between voice and suffering been better captured than in Elaine Scarry's *The Body in Pain* (Oxford University Press, 1985). There in an essay on torture she explains that torturers derive their power from the voices of the tortured. The object of torture is not to exact a confession or to learn information, but rather to force the tortured person to accuse her very self. This happens when the body, so broken with pain, is unable to keep the voice from submitting to the phony power of the torturer. The aim of torture, then, is to tear the voice from its body and force it to capitulate to the torturer. Tragically after the capitulation, the tortured body is left voiceless. Betrayal is the object of those who deliberately cause suffering. Those who want to make another person suffer recognize that the voice is the way people keep body and soul together. They torture to make their victim's voice become the accuser.

Scarry notes that for the tortured person, the wound most difficult to heal is the voice. For this reason, Amnesty International assists victims of torture, unable out of shame to tell their narratives, to read and understand their own records so that they may articulate one day the truth of the atrocities against them. Scarry convincingly demonstrates the centrality of the human voice in attaining healing integration. This is why we must listen to one who is suffering.

Scarry highlights how silencing is a physically and personally destructive act. When the voice is not allowed to express itself, the sufferer finally loses the most integral way by which she can communicate and remain in contact with the community that supports her. Studies show us not only the therapeutic function the voice has in the life of the sufferer, but conversely the compounded suffering that occurs when that voice is ignored, lost, or silenced. For, like torture itself, the act of silencing a sufferer (or worse, of making a suffering person speak against herself) is a violent action.

Although much has been written on the meaning of suffering, those writings violate the sufferer yet again to the extent that they ignore, replace, or translate the sufferer's own voice without heeding exactly what the narrator has communicated. I am reminded, for instance, of the Christian insistence on translating the suffering of the Jews in the Holocaust. And I recall the suffering of homosexuals and gypsies in the Holocaust, who were never even given a hearing.

"ORDINARY" SUFFERING

Such violence occurs again and again in commonplace situations. Consider two ordinary stories about a friend of mine and her daughter, both of whom are suffering these days. Connie is a lawyer, a devoted mother of three, whose middle daughter Maureen is eleven years old and fighting leukemia. She told me the story of a little eight-year-old in the bed next to her daughter, also suffering from leukemia. When the nurse came in to give her an injection, the girl cried, "I'm afraid." "No, you're not afraid; you are a big girl," said the nurse in contradiction, giving her the injection. After the nurse left, my friend Connie went over to the girl's mother and said, "Excuse me, but I would never let a nurse or doctor contradict my child. Things are bad enough; she should not have to conform her suffering to the nurse's well-meaning efficiency."

The second story is like the first. Maureen, suffering from punctured lungs, has been living for several weeks with tubes in her chest. In her room, an older women with a similar catheter asked her, "Honey, when they put that thing in your chest did they say that you would experience 'discomfort'?" "Yes," she responded. "You know, discomfort is sitting in a wooden chair for twenty minutes or wearing tight shoes. That thing hanging out of your chest isn't discomfort; it's living hell." Little Maureen, facing leukemia, found in that woman someone who knew her suffering. But those who translated her suffering as "discomfort" were unable to listen, let alone understand the little girl's living hell.

CHAPTER TWENTY

Moral Theology Today

T welve years ago while I was doing my doctorate at the Gregorian University, a fellow American Jesuit asked me how my dissertation was going. I said okay and he was surprised. He believed that since I was working in moral theology that I would have already finished, "It is after all, nothing more than codes and rules." I was surprised by the impression. Is that what he thought moral theology was?

In a manner of speaking, he was right. Until the Second Vatican Council, moral theology remained for nearly three centuries a code of conduct; its hallmark for being right was that it rarely changed. For this reason, Henry Davis' *Moral and Pastoral Theology* was found in all seminaries and was probably the most referred text in moral theology for nearly thirty years. Moral theology was always reliable: it told us what was right or wrong, and it was always the same everywhere.

So what has happened? How did we go from a universal code of certainty to the present situation in which there is considerable debate, great uncertainty, and terrible complexity? To understand how we got where we are today, I propose that we consider some of the changes that have occurred as a result of the renewal from the Second Vatican Council. Here I offer a list of ten changes.

1. *The aim of moral theology: From avoiding sin to becoming a disciple.* Before the Council, moral theology had the simple but specific task to determine what was permitted and what

was sinful. Ascetical theology, or what we today call spirituality, had the task of building up character. Thus in the 1930s the moral theologian Thomas Slater wrote about the aim of moral theology: "its primary object is to teach the priest how to distinguish what is sinful from what is lawful . . . it is not intended for edification nor for the building up of character."

With this aim, the moral theologian was like the scribe in the New Testament who knew the law well. Davis, for instance, wrote, ". . . it is precisely about law that Moral Theology is concerned. It is not a mirror of perfection." Before the Council, then, moral theologians wrote about laws and sin, not about character or spirituality. If we remember the first principle of conscience, to do good and to avoid evil, moral theology took care to avoid evil; ascetical theology, to do good.

The Second Vatican Council Fathers criticized this way of doing moral theology: "Special attention needs to be given to the development of moral theology. Its scientific exposition should be more thoroughly nourished by scriptural teaching. It should show the nobility of the Christian vocation of the faithful, and their obligation to bring forth fruit in charity for the life of the world (*Optatam Totius*, 16)." The Council called on moral theologians to change their aim. To keep people from sin was not enough; they had to help illuminate their way of following the Lord, by reflecting on what it meant to be a disciple of Jesus Christ.

2. Jesus Christ: From judge to leader in faith. With its emphasis on sin and law and not on perfection, moral theology prior to the Council considered Jesus Christ primarily as Judge of the Last Day. When the Council issued its call to discipleship, however, moral theology looked on Jesus Christ as the One who goes before us. In particular, Bernard Häring's three volume work, *The Law of Christ,* afforded moral theologians the opportunity to reconsider our relationship with Jesus in three ways. First, the aim of moral theology would no longer be to avoid sin but to follow Jesus. Second, our moral worth would no longer be measured by singular actions, but rather by our whole lives as disciples. Third, the moral life would then be relational: Christ calling each of us and we responding in grace by following Him.

3. *The text: From manuals to the Scriptures.* This turn to Jesus led moral theologians to see (as the early Church once saw) that the Gospels must be the guide for our moral journey in the footsteps of Christ. But, for three centuries prior to the Council, the most consulted text for moral theologians was not the Gospels, but rather the handbooks or, as they were commonly called, the "manuals" of their predecessors. In fact, a moral theologian's achievement was to publish a commentary on a great predecessor's manual.

Three effects resulted from this shift from manuals to the Gospels. First, since one generation after another of moral theologians—or manualists, as they were called—commented on their predecessor's works, continuity was key in this self-perpetuating cycle. By turning to the Gospels, moral theology was now faced with the new. In particular, the Good News demanded that the revelation of Jesus had to be translated into some tangible significance for the here and now. Second, while the manuals evaluated human action, the Gospels emphasized interiority. Third, the turn to the Scriptures caused moral theologians to change their writing style. In the history of Christian literature nothing is more boring than the manuals of moral theology and in that same history nothing is richer than the parables of Jesus. The continuous, universal, unchanging teachings of the manuals no longer seemed attractive, nor for that matter, all that necessary for salvation. In their stead, the Gospels led many to realize that moral theology had to reflect much more on the interior life.

4. *Charity: From periphery to heart of the moral life.* Before the Council, charity was usually considered a supererogatory virtue, that is, as something we could choose to do that would bring reward. Charity was something extra; it was not required. Moreover, we exercised charity toward those worse off than we were. But because charity depended completely on our choice, those who were worse off

than we were, remained that way. For this reason, in the 1960s a slogan appeared about what was due to the poor: "Justice, not charity."

Ironically just as those in social justice were abandoning charity, Gerard Gilleman wrote *The Primacy of Charity in Moral Theology* for moral theologians. In a return to Thomas Aquinas, Gilleman showed that charity was central to the moral life. In particular, he uncovered the centrality charity played, not in exterior acts of generosity, but in the interior love for God and neighbor. Charity went, then, from being elective and on the periphery to being necessarily at the heart of moral theology. Moreover, in the Gospels charity is the moral measure of the interior life: if we have charity, we are good; if not, we are bad. If we have not charity, regardless of how right our exterior actions are, even suffering death for the faith, we are nothing.

This emphasis on charity led moral theologians to the notion of the fundamental option. Simply put, the fundamental option asks whether we have charity: is our basic disposition directed to the love of God and neighbor or not?

5. *The understanding of sin: From "what I have done" to "what I have failed to do."* The manuals in moral theology were always writing on sin. Slater again reminds us what those manuals were about: "They deal with what is of obligation under pain of sin; they are books of moral pathology." But, as the aim of moral theology changed, so did its notion of sin.

Before the Council, sin concerned what we did. In confession, we recalled what we did. After the Council, we returned to a Gospel notion of sin, like Matthew 25, where those cast into hell fire are those who have not fed the hungry, not clothed the naked, not comforted the sick nor welcomed the stranger. By turning to the Scriptures, we began to see sin not as what we did, but more compellingly as what we failed to do.

This shift in understanding entered into our prayer life particularly in the penitential rite of the liturgy. In this shift, the Church began again to describe sin in terms of our failure in discipleship. This notion of sin, as failing both to follow the Lord and to respond to our neighbor, we now realize as we saw above, was developed by many early theologians, like Gregory, Bernard, and Thomas.

Becoming better or growing in the virtues or becoming a disciple of Christ was no longer simply something extra. Before the Council, moral theology was about keeping us from becoming worse; after the Council, moral theology was about making sure we responded to Christ in charity. This latter insight was the one founded on the Scriptures. Since charity was required now, hearts that failed to respond to Christ were considered sinful.

6. *Expanding the use of the principle of totality.* Since the thirteenth century moral theologians used some form of this principle, as they did in the question of capital punishment. They wrote, for instance, that as a bad limb could be removed for the sake of a healthy body, likewise an individual malefactor could be killed for the sake of the common good. Curiously, outside of a specific social issue like this one, the principle was used in a restrictive way.

In medical matters, the principle appears in the case of saving a life by removing an organ. The harm done to one organ is justified by the benefit the action provides to the whole body. Likewise, the principle was used for vaccines. If a vaccine is actually the direct introduction of the disease into a person, how can we permit it? Theologians argued that the action of temporary direct harm is justified by the overall health of the body that in the long run is protected. Thus, medical problems only referred to the principle in cases limited to parts of one person's body in relationship to that particular body.

In the 1960s transplants prompted a new discussion. Could we remove one organ from one body for the sake of another body? Many moral theologians thought that the principle of totality could be used. They acknowledged that to remove an unhealthy organ, for instance, an appendix, to save one's body is different from removing one's kidney to save another's body. But they referred to the case of capital punishment and thus stretched the limits of totality in medical ethics.

Though it had been used restrictively in medical ethics, totality had not been used at all in sexual ethics. But in the 1960s the principle became invoked on the matter of birth control. Could one use a contraceptive for a marital act and still argue that if the couple sincerely intended to have children, then the totality of their marital acts were actually procreative and not contraceptive? This argument made sense to many experts who sat on the papal commission to consider birth control. But in *Humanae vitae* Pope Paul VI rejected this use of the principle.

Still the principle was invoked again. Could a woman whose uterus was scarred after several pregnancies undergo minor surgery to protect herself from a dangerous future pregnancy? Here a function would be suppressed for her health. Could a couple unable to have children utilize reproductive technologies even if it meant that the act of procreation occurred outside of the marital act? Could the couple argue that if they engage regularly in marital acts that all the acts leading up to the reproductive technology are themselves procreative? In *Donum vitae,* however, Pope John Paul II rejected this use of the principle.

Nonetheless, the principle continues to be invoked on a variety of topics. This is due to three reasons. First, we have today a more holistic understanding of the person. Though before the Council we spoke almost always about actions rather than persons, by looking at the person we began to see that one act does not make a person. Second, by our turn to interiority, we found a way of unifying one act to another, that is, through the intention. The end that a person intends through a series of related actions can often be evaluated through the principle of totality. Finally, contemporary moral theologians argue that unless all circumstances, intentions, and objects are weighed, then we cannot measure properly whether an intended way of acting is moral or not. Totality demands that we not exclude morally relevant information. Not surprisingly, then, the principle of totality has become, as John Mahoney remarks in his celebrated *The Making of Moral Theology,* the most important principle in moral theology.

7. *No longer a clerical profession.* Totality also prompted a change in the faculties of moral theology. For centuries, like most of

theology, moral theology was a subject taught to seminarians by priests. This is definitely no longer the case. No longer depending on three centuries of texts that were accessible to only a few, moral theology with its interest in Scripture, discipleship, and interiority attracted lay people into its study and now into its practice. As a result, more lay people, both men and women, are investing five to seven years of graduate study in moral theology in order to become moral theologians. These lay people are not only men.

Indeed, as a singularly clerical discipline, moral theology was about "moral pathology" and not surprisingly, because some of the most intimate knowledge that priests had of the laity was in the confession of sinfulness. That knowledge became foundational to the moral theologian. It became the "stuff" about which moral theologians taught. Now that students and teachers in the field of moral theology are both clerical and lay and, now that the subject matter of moral theology is not only our sins but more importantly our goals, moral theology covers every dimension of human life.

8. *New concerns about relativism.* By leaving the manuals' emphasis on specific external acts, concern arose in moral theology about relativism. Indeed, relativism is probably the greatest danger that the new encyclical *Veritatis Splendor* warns against. Relativism is the denial of the claims of objective truth to any degree. For instance, if equality is an objective truth, and I without any justifying reason ignore equality and show favoritism, I act as a relativist.

The manuals' emphasis on universal and unchanging truth gave the impression that they were completely against relativism. But, after the Council, moral theologians began asking, if we hold to the rules of the manuals regardless of circumstances, can we possibly know the objectively right? For instance, in the example above, if equality is an objective truth are we relativists if we say that eight-year-old children ought to be treated differently than twenty-three-year-old children? It seems, as a matter of fact, that if we don't entertain circumstances like age then we may not find the objectively right answer after all. Hard-fixed rules do not guarantee against relativism.

Certainly, the manuals' universal and unchanging rules prevented people from doing whatever they wanted. But though they prevented arbitrariness, they did not guarantee objectivity; by ignoring the circumstances of situations, they excluded important information for determining what was morally demanded in a situation. To protect us from relativism, then, contemporary moral theologians warn against being arbitrary, on the one hand, and against having a complacent belief in unyielding rules, on the other hand. In between they propose prudence as the standard for moral reasoning that includes circumstances and rejects subjectivity.

9. *A new appreciation for conscience.* The Church has always had a strange relationship with conscience. Probably the greatest insight into conscience in the middle ages came from Thomas Aquinas who argued that when we go against our conscience we sin and (against Peter Lombard) that we should rather die excommunicated than violate our conscience.

But for three centuries, though moral theologians argued for the primacy of conscience, they also made sure that everyone had the same consciences. This was a major accomplishment, achieved by first considering the good conscience to be only that which "avoided sin" and second by determining exactly what were the sinful acts. Every formed conscience knew about stealing, killing, lust, and so on, and anything beyond the category of these sins was less important for conscience.

In the turn to discipleship, we ask in conscience not only what is evil, but what is good. In doing that, the task of forming and following the conscience becomes more complex and, obviously, more personal. Yet in order to find right ways of responding to Christ, our consciences must seek not only personal, but also objectively right answers. To offer the conscience a guide for finding that which is personally and morally appropriate, moral theologians turn to the virtues.

10. *A return to virtues.* Moral theologians have returned to the ethics of Aquinas, Augustine, and Aristotle to study the virtues. In particular the virtues of justice, fidelity, and prudence have become

progressively the subject of extensive reflection. These virtues help us to order our interior lives so that our external actions express our personal and moral convictions.

Acquiring the virtue of justice is important because as we try to treat one another equally we begin to understand the enormous degree of diversity that distinguishes us as persons, families, cultures, nations, and tribes. Fidelity arises simply because though we must treat one another equally we must also respect particular ties that exist on account of our relatedness to one another through blood, marriage, the sacraments, love, and friendship. In order to grow in the virtues of justice and fidelity, we need prudence to teach us which steps to take and when and where and how to take them. Prudence's attentiveness to circumstances enables us to find exactly what is right behavior in the here and now for a person following in the footsteps of Christ.

In sum, if we want to know where we are in moral theology today, we are exactly where Slater said we should not be: working on the building of character. Certainly, Slater may have been right. But for the time being, it seems to the contrary that Kevin Kelly is right when he describes the *New Directions in Moral Theology* as "the challenge of being human." In answering that challenge moral theologians invite us to turn our attention to the virtues.

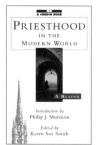
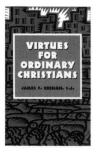

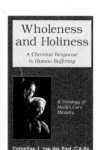